SpringerBriefs in Philosophy

More information about this series at http://www.springer.com/series/10082

Ranjan K. Ghosh

Essays in Literary Aesthetics

 Springer

Ranjan K. Ghosh
Indian Council of Philosophical Research
New Delhi, Delhi, India

ISSN 2211-4548   ISSN 2211-4556   (electronic)
SpringerBriefs in Philosophy
ISBN 978-981-13-2459-8   ISBN 978-981-13-2460-4   (eBook)
https://doi.org/10.1007/978-981-13-2460-4

Library of Congress Control Number: 2018953703

This Springer imprint is published by the registered company Springer Nature Singapore Pte Ltd.
The registered company address is: 152 Beach Road, #21-01/04 Gateway East, Singapore 189721,
Singapore

For my daughter
Stutee
who insisted on my
writing this book

Preface

The project aims at revisiting some of the philosophical issues related to meaning and interpretation of literary text and the nature of emotions one confronts in it. Contemporary aesthetical discourse is increasingly addressed to some of these issues that continue to be the hunting ground for philosophers of analytical persuasion, in particular. The identification of the literary meaning or interpretation with intention has met with stiff opposition with the advent of the New Criticism and its doctrinal position of "the intentional fallacy" as argued by Wimsatt Jr. and Beardsley (1946). An important consequence of this criticism has been to deny any privileged access to the literary text that might be claimed by the author of the text. In recent years, Steven Knapp and Walter Michael (1992) have developed a defence of intentionalism though it is not explicitly directed against Wimsatt and Beardsley who argue against the notion of *authorial* intention. The latter view of anti-intentionalism involves holding the text as having its meaning embodied in it that is directly discoverable by the reader or critic by giving it a "close reading". The assumption here is that there is but only a *single* unalterable meaning which the reader should aim at. However, another variant of anti-intentionalism that is commonly associated with Post-structuralism disagrees with meaning-*monism* on the one hand and yet argues against authorial intention, on the other. Rather, one can speak of a plurality of meanings accordingly as each reader is able to make sense of the text. It has been held by some thinkers like Terry Eagleton that meaning is "produced" differently for different readers depending on the form of social life one belongs to. Indeed, an overview of the history of modern literary theory seems to indicate the following three stages: a preoccupation with the author (Romanticism and the Nineteenth Century), an exclusive concern with the text (New Criticism) and a marked shift of attention to the reader over recent years.

In a recent paper, John Searle (1994) has claimed that the distinction between sentence meaning and speaker meaning is relevant to our understanding of the meaning of a literary text. On his view, the conventional meaning has an independent status and should not be confused with the speaker meaning. The main thrust of Searle's argument seems to be that what makes language or sentences meaningful is the satisfiability condition of the conventional rules of grammar and syntax even if such occurrence comes about *by chance*. This is an interesting argument that needs to be gone into carefully. We also have to look at this argument from the standpoint of Knapp and Michael for whom the meaning of a poem must be identified with the poet's intention. How do we understand the distinction between sentence meaning and speaker meaning in the context of literary text? Some of the other broader questions that we need to address here are as follows: What is a literary text? What do we understand by the concept of intention in the context of literary text, given the fact that there are and can be various senses in which one talks about intention? How do we understand the distinction between sentence meaning and speaker meaning? What bearing will such a distinction have in the context of literary text and its interpretation? How do we understand the distinction between author's intention and the *intentionality* of the literary text? Can there be "intention less" language at all? How do we interpret a literary text without having regard to the notion of intention?

A literary text is also interpreted in terms of the emotion(s) it embodies. Are the feelings experienced in a literary text *real*? Further, when we feel pity for a character in a novel, or experience fear in response to some incident narrated in the novel, it makes sense to ask: Are these responses of the *same* kind as those that we experience in *real* life? In real-life situations, we *believe* that the person we feel pity for is not a fictional character. On the other hand, the character we feel pity for in a novel is *fictional*, and not real. So, are such reactions to a work of art real; or, are they merely *make-believe*? In short, what is the nature of our psychological reactions to a fiction? This question has come in for critical discussion in recent years. Interestingly, this question assumes importance mainly in the context of narrative arts and not so much in respect of other arts such as painting and sculpture.

Christopher New (1999) points out that in real-life situations, there are three features characteristic of *fear*: (a) belief that some real being is in danger, (b) psychological situations such as quickened pulse and sweating palms, and (c) the behavioural disposition to escape the danger. But when the reaction of fear arises in the mind in response to a novel, we do *not* believe that what we are responding to is an actual being, nor is it accompanied by our behavioural disposition to escape, though it is quite natural to experience our quickened pulse, sweating palms, etc. The point that Christopher New raises here is that our psychological response to fiction is not accompanied by belief in the reality of the character or situation to which such response is directed. On the other hand, our responses in the context of real-life situations have their home in the belief about the reality or actuality of the object of such responses. Are such responses only "make-believe"? Or, even if the responses were real, are they "irrational"? Kendall Walton (1978), for example, takes the position that the characters in a novel are *fictional* and do not exist in real life and so we *pretend* to ourselves the reactions such as fear and pity towards these characters. The theory that our psychological responses to a work of art are "make-believe" cannot explain why one experiences the sensations and other bodily changes. This theory also cannot explain the fact that after we have put away the novel, we describe our psychological reactions in the same way as we do in real-life situations. Moreover, in the case of comic emotion, we do not pretend to ourselves that we are laughing; our laughter is *real*. Thus the thesis of "make-believe" reaction seems vulnerable on many counts. Alex Neil (1991) points to some of these points. Richard Shusterman (1988), William Dowling (1985), George Wilson (1991), I. Dilman (1995), R.M.J. Damman (1992), Peter McCormick (1988), Julian Mitchell (1973), and many others have carried on the discussion.

Now if it were argued that fictionality belongs to all literary works, then there would at once seem to arise opposition between literature and philosophy. Further, philosophers who hold the view that literature and philosophy can be combined will be under the burden of arguing that there is a very distinctive sense in which the talk about truth in literature is licit. What is that sense of "truth" in the context of literary arts? The questions that will engage us here are as follows: What is the nature of emotions we experience in literature? Are these emotions "make-believe"? Why then do we experience bodily sensations such as fast heartbeat and sweating if these emotions are "make-believe? Are these emotions then "irrational"? What is the sense of "truth" in literature, which is fictional in character?

In the following chapters, some of these questions have been gone into from a critical perspective. Many of these issues are being discussed in a large number of publications that have appeared in recent years. Indeed, much thinking needs to go into some of these issues. The present work was done during the period I was awarded the Senior Fellowship by the Indian Council of Philosophical Research (ICPR). I am also deeply indebted to the ICPR for their kind permission to get it published.

I am grateful to Professor S.R. Bhatt, Chairman, ICPR, for his inspiring support to me in carrying out the work. I would also take this opportunity to sincerely thank Professor Mrinal Miri for his valuable help and suggestions for this research project. I would like to acknowledge the help and assistance provided to me by the Delhi University South Campus library. Also, I would like to place on record my sincere gratitude to the Springer Publishing Company for agreeing to publish this work. And now, if I might end it on a slightly personal note, I fondly recall the long hours of discussions with my wife Preeti on several topics I have dealt with in this book.

New Delhi, India   Ranjan K. Ghosh

Contents

About the Author

Ranjan K. Ghosh, PhD, was till recently Senior Fellow of the Indian Council of Philosopical Research (ICPR), and previously taught philosophy at the University of Delhi and North Bengal University, West Bengal, where he also served as Head, Department of Philosophy. He also worked as Senior Research Scientist (UGC) at Delhi University. He was sometime Director ICPR and held Visiting Professorship in the department of Philosophy at Hyderabad Central University and in College of Art, New Delhi where he taught aesthetics and art criticism. He has published several books and research articles in peer-refereed journals including the *British Journal of Aesthetics* and *The Journal of Aesthetics and Art Criticism*. Professor Ghosh is the current Managing Editor of the *Journal of Indian Council of Philosophical Research*. An artist, and art critic, he writes regularly on art and aesthetics in popular art magazines and journals and is based in New Delhi. He also edits and regularly brings out a literary quarterly "Dhvani". And being committed to the idea of education through art he holds workshops/classes on Sundays with young school children to motivate them.

Chapter 1
Providing the Context

Abstract The chapter begins with a brief overview of the contemporary trends in analytic approach to deal with philosophical questions concerning art, in general, and literature, in particular. Such concern with the analyses and clarification of concepts has played an important role though it has been argued that such an approach has serious limitations in coming out with fresh insights into the nature of art and literature. While there is an attempt to bring out the salient points arrived at by such analytic approach, it also warrants the need to adopt a more comprehensive and synoptic approach. It is thus necessary to understand the creative product as an autonomous domain. This also points to questions concerning the literary text and its meaning, its relation to life and morals and aesthetic emotions and their experience.

Keywords Analytic approach · Anti-intentionalism · Definition · Classificatory and evaluative senses

Aesthetics as a serious and critical reflection on issues relating to the landscape of beauty and art is a latecomer in the Anglo-Saxon world of philosophical discourse. Such discourse has gained momentum in the latter half of the twentieth century.[1] Most of the thinkers that came before this period had remained focused mainly on the attempt to formulate a definition of art or beauty. An exercise of this nature was premised on the belief that the task involved finding an *essential* quality or characteristic that must be present in all particular instances of art and beauty. This was quite in line with the legacy of the Western tradition that goes back to the times of Socrates and Plato who addressed the problem of the particulars and universals. By around the mid-twentieth century, the edifice of such thinking came to be challenged as Wittgenstein in his later works (notably, "Philosophical Investigation") came to seriously question this mode of philosophical thinking, namely, essentialism. The influence of such thinking became pervasive as many young philosophers were inspired by Wittgenstein's pathbreaking approach. This motley group of

---

[1] Questions relating to the nature of art and beauty date back though to the times of Socrates and Plato.

philosophers, who came to be known as analytic philosophers, carried forward the strains of such ideas into other fields of enquiry including philosophical aesthetics.

Morris Weitz (1956) is one of the earliest philosophers to call in question the traditional philosopher's concern with the definition of art. According to him, there is a conceptual muddle when one seeks a definition of art in terms of some common quality that may be claimed to be possessed by all the instances of art. The analytic philosopher, who is deeply influenced by the anti-essentialism of the later Wittgenstein, regards the concept "art" as an "open-textured" concept. For him, finding a definition of art in terms of an essential property or characteristic is "logically vain". The concept "art" and a host of other natural concepts are like concepts "game", and "language" which are open-textured as no strictly necessary and sufficient conditions can be laid down for them.

Morris Weitz puts forward two main arguments in this regard. First, on inspection one can find nothing common among all the various range of products and activities that form the sub-concepts under the rubric concept "art". Painting, sculpture, music, poetry, cinema, novel, etc. represent a vast and diverse range of activities in terms of their medium and the manner of their execution. This compares well with the concept "games" or "language" as there is nothing common among all the various games (e.g. ball games, card games, etc.) or language (e.g. Sanskrit, Spanish, Tamil, Hindi, etc.). These are called by the same common name, "games" or "language", not because, but in spite of, there being nothing common among them. Second, while attempting to find a definition of art, we will be looking at only a selected group of works that are generally regarded as paradigmatic cases of art. Now, even if we find some common characteristic or quality that runs through all these excellent cases of art (say, Shakespeare's drama, Picasso's painting, Ravi Shankar's Sitar recital, Tagore's poetry and so on), that would count for the "criterion of excellence" and not a defining property for all works of art or the "criterion of recognition". In other words, the "criterion of excellence" cannot pass off as the "criterion of recognition" or defining characteristic.[2]

It is important to note that the concept "art" is an "open" concept because newer sub-concepts under it may be added in future. For example, "installation art" is a recent addition under the rubric term "art". Thus, we cannot foreclose on the possibility of newer sub-concepts that are hitherto unknown. For that matter, "street play" and "rap music" are new additions to the known list of art forms. In such a scheme of things, it is quite futile to attempt pegging down a common definition that would be valid for all works of art. How do we then respond to the question: "What is art"?

Now, it is further suggested by Weitz (1956) that the question "What is art?" be supplanted by the question "what sort of concept is art?" This is a turning point in the contemporary discourse on art and opens up a number of issues for the philosopher, who is given to analytical persuasion. Rather than engaging in the task of defining art it calls for analysis and unpacking of the concept of art. Gallie (1956),

---

[2]Weitz (1956) draws a distinction between "criterion of excellence" and "criterion of recognition".

Kennick (1958), Hampshire (1970), McDonald (1965), Margolis (1980, 217), Mandelbaum (1979, 446), Beardsley (1978, 6–24) and many others found a fertile philosophical hunting ground for analyses.

The analytic philosopher is able to clearly demarcate an area of philosophical pursuit that is quite different from the domain of traditional aesthetics. Analytic aesthetics directs its focus on the *language* and *logic* of criticism. The age-old questions relating to the nature and definition of art and beauty get relegated to the background as a patent source of conceptual muddle. The problems that come for discussion are those that arise from the critical statements made about works of art. Analysis of the language for describing, interpreting and sometimes evaluating artworks occupies the centre stage of philosophical aesthetics. Also, the traditional definitions of art come under the scanner of close linguistic analysis. This quest for clarity by means of analysis of language coupled with the diction of anti-essentialism constitutes the bedrock of all *analytic* aesthetics.

There is another significant factor that must be taken note of in this context. Much of the arts in the twentieth century show quite a degree of waywardness in terms of moving away from earlier conventions and trends. This is perhaps more visibly marked in the plastic arts such as paintings and sculptures. Such art may often seem to resist or defy being subsumed under the accepted parameters of art. This begs the question as to the use of the term "art" for such instances of creative endeavour and outpouring. Cases of *Dada* art are a clear departure from everything hitherto known and designated as art.

The distinction between the "criterion of excellence" and "criterion of recognition" made by Morris Weitz also brings into focus a clear wedge between the *two* senses in which the term "art" is used: art in the *classificatory* sense and art as a *value* term. The implicit suggestion that is advanced here is that it may be possible to look for and find some common characteristics among all the various works that are lauded as excellent specimens of art. This cannot be said for all the things that come to be designated as art in its classificatory sense. Why should we call something as an instance of art at all? This question is quite different from the question: why do we call something as "good" or "excellent" work of art? For some of the analytic philosophers, the latter question is easier to answer: we can, as we often do, point to "x", "y" or "z" characteristic in a work of art to justify why it is to be regarded as good or excellent work of art. But why, in the first places, do we call something as art at all? This is where we come up against a conceptual muddle.

Now, some recent thinkers have questioned the very basis for the theory of two senses of art. Rowe (1991) joins issues with Weitz on this point and argues that the distinction between the two senses is "ill founded" and the definition of art "cannot be value-neutral". This argument is based on the following analysis of three types of noun words: (a) words such as knife or tin-opener; (b) words such as apple, mule etc.; and (c) words like rock, sawdust, etc. Now, knife and tin-opener are defined wholly or partially in terms of their function; apple and mule are *not* defined functionally, but they have socially accepted function; but, rock and sawdust do not fall in either category.

Rowe suggests that if we prefix the term "good" before these various noun words, it means differently in the cases such as the following: (a) good tin-opener, (b) good apple and (c) good rock. Cases of (a) and (b) behave in a way that would be very different from that at (c). A "good rock" will not make much sense unless we specify what it is good for or as. But a "good tin-opener" would be one that more efficiently does the *function* of cutting open the tin. Similarly a "good apple" would be one that fulfills the socially accepted function, that is, as more nutrient food. An apple that is not so tasty and nutrient would still be called an apple. For that matter, even a rotten apple would also be called an "apple", though it may be called a "good apple" if the purpose is to use it as a missile to scare away a political leader.

Now if we turn back to the case of tin-opener, it is *defined only in terms of its function* as a tin-cutter/opener. But what do we say about a tin-cutter or a vehicle that does not work or function at all? A rusted tin-cutter or a bogged down non-functional car that does not perform its defined function is called by that name only in a *derivative sense*. In other words, it derives its name from the evaluative sense of the term with reference to its defined function.

What Rowe says may be summarized as follows: (i) The term "art" in conjunction with the attributive "good" behaves in much the same way as do functionally defined terms such as tin-opener or car. These terms are defined only by the function for which they are produced. (ii) In the event of their being non-functional or not functioning as per requirement, they *derive* their meaning and usage from the *evaluative* sense in which they are held when fully functional. (iii) By pressing together these two points, he concludes that "art" has only *one* legitimate sense, that of its evaluative function. Works of art are created to fulfill certain function, and so long as this function is performed, the term "art" can be understood or regarded only in its *evaluative* sense; the classificatory sense ensues from this evaluative sense. For Rowe, the theory of the "two senses of art" falls through in view of the foregoing analysis. This seems to pave the way for the *possibility of a definition of art* in terms of the essential function it performs.

The thrust of Rowe's analyses is to map "art" as a functional concept so that for something to be called art it must achieve "a certain minimal standard" of the assigned function. When a thing is evaluated as "good art", it means it functions as art to an eminent degree. What goes to make it a case of "good art" is the same that goes to make it a case of "art" in the first place. The distinction between "art" and "good art" is only one of degree. The "classificatory" sense of art is parasitic on its "evaluative" sense. However there is one difficulty that arises here. One can never be sure of the acceptability or otherwise of the borderline cases of art.

We may now term to some inadequacies in Rowe's account of art as a functional concept. A basic question that may be asked here is, what is it for a work of art to function as art? Is there a clearly demarcated and universally accepted function of art? The comparison between tin-opener and art seems to break down on this account. Tin-openers have a clearly demarcated function, but art does not seem to have one. Further, is their one single function of art, or can we think of more than one function of art?

Rowe seems to suggested that the term "art" is used for an object that is "good to look at, listen to, i.e., for disinterested aesthetic contemplation in the widest sense", and its function is "to hold the interest of an audience". But there may be more ways than one to hold the interest of an audience. Further, the term "aesthetic contemplation" also stands in need of a clear and intelligible explanation. So there is quite undeniable difference between the clear cut tangible function of a tin-opener and that of an artwork which is rather amorphous to allow almost anything under the rubric term art.

One more important point is this. The function of a tin-opener can be assessed independently of the person that uses it. But how do we assert the function of an artwork independently of the person that responds to it? The same movie/painting is appreciated differently by different people; some may rate it very high on the basis of their own responses, while others may not find the same very satisfying. There is perhaps a degree of subjectivity based on one's own background and exposure to other works that comes into play. For that matter, appreciation of a work of art is a highly refined cultural enterprise.

Regardless of all its inadequacies that the functional analysis of art as presented by Rowe suffers from it does succeed in bringing home a point of considerable interest. There can be no exclusive "classificatory" sense of art independent of its "evaluative" sense. The sharp wedge drawn between the two senses of art by M. Weitz seems only an arbitrary division that does not take into account the substantial manner in which we *respond* to works of art. Our judgment with regard to a work of art is critically based on our *response* to the work. How can we refute this fact of experience? Interestingly, this is an area of concern that the analytic philosopher tends to shy away from for fear of being charged with psychologism. The moot point is how can we ignore or leave out of consideration the fulcrum of experience in a meaningful discourse on art? If art is not capable of giving us a special sort of *experience*, what is it that we are interested in it *for?*

Instead, M. Weitz seeks to make out a case for the wedge between the "two" senses of art by stressing on the logical futility of finding a definition of art in terms of common essence for all the things that are regarded as art in the "classificatory" sense. He, in fact, concedes that a definition in terms of a common essence would be possible if we take into account cases of art in the "evaluative" sense. Further, he goes on to invoke the Wittgenstein's notion of "family resemblance" to account for the "classificatory" sense of art: one can find and enumerate some commonly shared qualities (essences) among all the paradigm cases of art ("evaluative" sense) and say that the members under the "classificatory" sense of art bear "family resemblance" to these. According to Wittgenstein, "family resemblances" are sorts of resemblances that one might trace among members of the same family (say, in terms of eyes, nose, ears, hair and so on). The point of it is that these resemblances are *not* in respect of any one such common feature but is in respect of "strands of similarities" of qualities/features.

However, as some later thinkers (Mandelbaum 1979, 446) have pointed out, the notion of "family resemblance" itself is problematic and stands in need of further clarification. Do cases of resemblance between things quality as cases of "family resemblance"? Talking about "family resemblances" among the siblings, we know already that they are offsprings from the same parents. Turning to cases of art, in what sense do diverse things and activities such as paintings, sonatas, street corner plays, novels, etc. belong to the same "family"? For example, a calendar illustration may bear some resemblance to, say, some well-known painting in terms of certain outward features such as scenic ingredients, human figures, etc. which would not count as a case of "family resemblance". The thrust of the argument is that only when we know that members of a family are genetically connected that it makes sense to talk about "family resemblance". In the case of all the diverse objects and activities that claim the status of art, there is no genetic linkage. Perhaps, one might point out that Wittgenstein coined the term "family resemblance" as only a metaphor only to drive home the point that all the diverse things that are brought under the rubric term "art" bear such resemblances to the known characteristics/qualities to be found in paradigmatic instances of art rather than sharing any common *essence*. But that is not going too far in the business of finding a general definition of art.

It is in this context that the analyst in Rowe rightly calls a halt to distinguishing the two senses, and points out that "art" is a functional term that can be defined in terms of its *essential* function, that of becoming a candidate for disinterested contemplation. The broad argument is that a tin-opener is a tin-opener if it *functions* as a tin-opener, and art is art if it functions as art. We may, however, put a fine point on this. The function of tin-opener is to do something *for* us, but the function of art is to do something *to* us. For this reason one is a functional term but the other a value-laden term. Tin-cutters and art objects cannot be put in the same class of noun words as it is being claimed by M.R. Rowe. Hence, the argument that both these terms are definable in terms of their function seems a rather sweeping generalization. Our concern is with a value-laden term "art" and the nature of such value. Art does something to us and does so depending upon our own responsiveness to it.

It is interesting that just as M. Weitz shows overmuch concern with the "classificatory" sense of art, so does George Dickie (1971, 101) by steering clear of the "evaluative" sense of art in his attempt to define the term. His "institutional" analysis of art is based on the assumed possibility that all works of art share a common "essence", though of an unmanifest kind. His earliest formulation which though went through several amendments is as follows:

A work of art in the classificatory sense is (i) an artefact (ii) upon which some person or persons, acting on behalf of a social institution (the art world), have conferred the status of candidate for appreciation.

A significant emendation subsequently carried out by Dickie in the modified formulation is to drop the idea of conferring on the work the status of "candidate for appreciation" and to hold that the artefact is created for the "art world". Catherine Lord (1987) rightly points out that "art world" is used by Dickie as a proper name rather than as a general term. An implication that follows from this is that this art world has a fixed reference of indexicality rather than as a general term. An implication that follows is that this art world has a fixed reference or *indexicality* rather than to be used as a general term. This in turn would bring in a sense of "*arbitrariness*" with regard to the decision of the "art world".

Dickie's analysis seems to have been a throwback from several of the significant developments in the field of visual arts over the past decades. The various "movements" including "Dadaism" that followed in Europe in the early decades of the twentieth century and ever since demonstrate sharp and radical departures from the conventional modes of visual art. So much contemporary art has come to be viewed as waywardness in its practice. Dickie's formulation has the flexibility to be responsive to such a situation and addresses the issue as to how certain suspects manage to wrest the title of art for themselves notable among them being Marcel Duchamp's "Fountain" (a castaway urinal).

While it may be true that too restrictive a definition of art would find it difficult to accommodate such waywardness in the phenomena of art, a too wide and sweeping definition would also remain quite inadequate. Duchamp's "Fountain" and many such unconventional works do get designated as art objects. But even after being told how certain things get classified under, one may still meaningfully ask, as Tilghman (1984) does in his book under the same title, "But is it art?" which is "a demand for explanation of the thing as art". This is indeed not made clear by the attempt made by Dickie in his "Institutional Theory" of art. What this theory does is to show *how* the "art world" decides to accept or reject things as art; it does not provide an *explanation* for this.

In their attempts to analyse art, both M. Weitz and G. Dickie presuppose that the distinction between two senses, evaluative and classificatory, must be kept sharply apart. By focusing on the classificatory sense, art is regarded as a value-neutral term which would be amenable to analysis. Quite clearly, value terms pose a challenge to the analytic thinker who remains obsessively focused on the logic of language.

In recent years, a more interesting approach towards understanding art has been made by Goran Hermeren (1995, 269). While writing from the perspective of analytic philosophy as he does, he seeks to analyse the concept in relation to life. He holds that art can be understood in various different ways. He goes on to distinguish three different "models" for understanding the interplay between art and life. Two of these models are more commonly accepted (a) that of holding works of art as *objects of meditation* and (b) regarding them as vehicles of *communication.*

A *third model* is (c) oriented towards gaining an *insight into life* by means of works of art. His main thrust is on working out interpretations into the realism of *intertextual* relations. This approach widens out the scope of interpretation such that it may enrich one's experience of life through the encounter with the work of art. Meaning of a work is to be experienced directly and nondiscursively. This had been earlier affirmed by the well-known thinker Susanne K. Langer (1953, 40) who drew a clear distinction between "discursive" and "presentational" symbol while identifying art with the latter. However, Hermeren makes no direct reference to this fact.

Hermeren's approach to this distinctive character of art to "Show, exemplify, express…" (Hermeren 1995, June) something without saying, questioning or asserting it in a way falls in line with the functional analysis of art. Further, it opens out the way for *multiple* interrelations of a work of art in terms of *possible* intentions of the artist rather than the assumed actual intention of the artist. Art, for him, enriches our experience by providing a better understanding about life in general. However, a caveat seems necessary here. He connects art with experience but not in the full blooded sense in which such experience is to be regarded as a distinctive class by itself that would be quite different from various other sorts of experiences.

Oswald Hanfling (1995), while having noted the waywardness of the concept of art to which M. Weitz responds by claiming that art is indefinable, contends that "the ultimate survivor… to make sense of the concept, is aesthete satisfaction". He argues that the basic motivation for which human beings engage in creative pursuit is based on this definite purpose of deriving a special kind of satisfaction. Hanfling's proposed *functional* definition of art is as follows. "A work of art is an artifact of a kind whose main function is to provide aesthetic satisfaction to others" (Hanfling 1995, January).

Hanfling's analysis has the implication that it is possible to draw a distinction between, say, "knife" and "art", in spite of Rowe having argued that the two such terms belong to the same class and, therefore, comparable in terms of both being defined in terms of their function. According to Hanfling, a knife cannot be defined only in terms of its function; it should also resemble a traditionally working knife. But not so with the term "art", its function of providing aesthetic satisfaction represents both necessary and sufficient condition of art. New cases of art are often marked by clear departure from the tradition, yet the guiding principle for including them under art is their capacity to give aesthetic satisfaction.

The point to note here is that aesthetic satisfaction may be provided by any artefact as well as nature. Needless to say that *all* cases of aesthetic satisfaction are not cases of art though the reverse is always true. Significantly enough, Hanfling provides a perspective that clearly breaks off from the object-centric view of art. This must be viewed in the backdrop of the approach and stance taken by the analytic aesthetics of not granting a special and independent status to the "aesthetic" for fear of having to deal with the category of the mental which must remain elusive to any analysis. The analyst's main concern is with our talk about some concrete and tangible objects (such as, works of art) rather than with our *experience* of them. The analytic philosopher generally overlooks that *nature* also provides aesthetic satisfaction that often comes *before* one has had occasion to confront objects of art in terms of aesthetic satisfaction. This is not vacuous as the aesthetic can be understood independently of art.

Following its general line of approach, the analytic philosopher mainly addresses the discourse about *art*. This is based on the assumption that only what is given objectively is reducible into language. On the other hand, "aesthetic value" that has to do with one's experience transcends the object of art. And given the analytic philosopher's preoccupation with language, he finds it difficult to come to terms with such experience of satisfaction that as claimed as of aesthetic value. This is also perhaps the reason why the idea of art as a functional term does not find favour with the majority of aestheticians in the analytic persuasion. For example, W.E. Kennick (Mind 1058) clearly rejects such an approach. And M. Weitz does not consider this possibility at all while arguing that it is logically futile to find a definition of art in terms of some common characteristics.

Now attempts made by Rowe and Hanfling are extremely significant as this provides for a critique of the hard core analytic trend in aesthetics. It can be legitimately claimed that the concerns of aesthetics go beyond the problems that arise in critical discourse about art. Richard Shusterman rightly points out that "in analytic aesthetics the bias toward art and neglect of nature is particularly pronounced" (Shusterman 1989, 6). For that matter, analytic philosophers by and large shun the question of evaluation damning it as what gives rise to a conceptual muddle in asking for general rules and canons by which such evaluative statements could be made.

This way of questioning and debunking the possibility of evaluative judgments about art can be seen in the views of thinkers like Stuart Hampshire (1970) and Margaret McDonald (1965). Hampshire draws a contrast between moral acts and works of art on the ground that the latter being gratuitous are not amenable to any rules while moral acts are characterized by rules and canons. Margaret McDonald compares aesthetic appraisal statements to legal verdicts. A legal verdict cannot be said to be "true" or "false"; one may argue for their being valid or invalid. Underlying such arguments is the claim that every work of art is "unique" in the sense of being "unrepeatable". Interestingly, this view about uniqueness of a work of art is criticized by Mary Mothersill (1967) who argues that even moral acts are not repeatable, and, therefore, each moral act should be considered as "unique" in the *sense* in which Hampshire makes the point. According to her, however, there is a sense in which every work of art is unique because it is "hard to describe, and that no description, as a matter of logic, is identical with the work itself" (Mothersill 1967). As for the point about art being "gratuitous" in nature and therefore not quite comparable to moral situations, it is pointed out by Joseph Margolis (1980) that even artistic creations embody the solution of its moral, intellectual and technical problems. This goes against the idea of art being "gratuitous". Often, it is in response to some problems of a technical nature for the artist to solve and resolve them.

However, the point about the distinction between moral and aesthetic judgment is a more serious one and needs to be gone into in some detail. The underlying assumption in such a distinction is that there is an exclusive domain of the aesthetic. M.C Beardsley comes out with a very insightful observation and analysis in this context. It has been said that the proper way to respond to a work of art is by adopting a special point of view which is quite different from other points of view such as moral, religious, sociological, historical. etc. Beardsley (1978) however is careful to draw a further distinction between "the aesthetic point of view" and "an aesthetic point of view". The former stands for a complex network of activities that would be relevant for gaining a response to the aesthetic value in the work. This would include interpreting a work with reference to works of other artists or other works by the same artist or in terms of the internal details of the work itself. Each of such response would count as "*an* aesthetic point of view", and such responses would add up to make for "*the* aesthetic point of view".

The implications of Beardsley's stand point are extremely important, relevant and far-reaching enough. It helps us to understand and perhaps to an extent, sort out various controversies in rejecting or acclaiming a particular work of art. In recent years, so much controversy has erupted over, say, Salman Rushdie's "The Satanic Verses", Deepa Mehta's film or M.F. Husain's nude "Mother India". Many people have felt alarmed at the possible religious, moral and sociological fall out of these works. Some of these creative artists stand punished by the audiences in terms of slander, severe criticism and even exile. Beardsley's attempt to sharpen the distinction between aesthetic and moral/other points of view helps one to understand and appreciate such divergent and disquieting views/appraisals about works of art.

Now by way of a critical assessment of Beardsley's perceptive viewpoint, we may imagine the following possible situations. (a) Suppose that a critic claims a work of art lacks any capacity to produce aesthetic delight. How can we falsify this claim? (b) Suppose that the aesthetic enjoyment from a work diminishes after a lapse of time. This often happens after one has had subsequent exposure to various other works. In such event, would our attribution of aesthetic value to the work turn out to be suspect? (c) Another possibility could be that a person is under the influence of LSD or some psychotropic drug and finds almost everything as a source of enjoyment. Beardsley does not pay much serious attention to (a) as he affirms his confidence in a trained critic who would be quite competent in this regard. As for (b) and (c), he modifies his view of "aesthetic value" as a function of aesthetic enjoyment when experienced "correctly and completely" (Beardsley 1978).

This brings as to another crucial point about the legitimacy of the aesthetic point of view. Is the aesthetic point of view justified or warranted in certain situational context? Many novels and films are based on the theme of human suffering, agony and violence. One may indeed question the legitimacy of adopting the aesthetic point of view to such events and situations that stand in need of practical solution and attention. This in a way sets up the aesthetic as what may seem antagonistic to the domain of morality. What is, however, of interest is that Beardsley's theory of the aesthetic point of view connects it back to the experiential content of art which proves to be the *bête noire* for the hardcore analytic philosopher who finds it hard to bring it under the lens of analysis.

Let us now turn to a brief critical review and assessment of what has come to be known as the analytic trend in philosophizing about art or analytic aesthetics. In the first place, it seems that the term "aesthetics" is a misnomer in this context as it stands truncated into what may be described only as analysis of our discourse about *art*. In other words, analytic trend in aesthetics is more in line with philosophy of art. It remains generally recalcitrant to an essentialist approach towards understanding the nature of art and holds that the term "art" does not stand for a set of necessary and sufficient condition or some *essence*. Just as the term "games" stands for a vast and diverse range of activities and may be understood in terms of "strands of similarities" or "family resemblances" among all these activities so that "art" be understood by way of "family resemblances" and not as characterized by some common "essence among all instances of it" (Weitz 1956). However, the notion of "family resemblance" itself is a composite of two terms "family" and "resemblance", and each has a different connotation. All cases of resemblance are not necessarily cases that fall under the same *family*. So to apply this composite term to cases of art is to beg the question whether and how they all constitute a family. We confront circularity even while using the notion of family resemblance. It clearly fails to be able to accommodate all the diverse and waywardly things that have come to be categorized as art. It also fails to answer as to why they are categorized as art.

Second, by way of a further strategy a distinction is drawn between the two senses of art: "classificatory" and "evaluative" senses. The argument is that even if it is possible to find some essence or common characteristic in respect of those cases that are bestowed with the honorific title "art" (i.e. evaluative sense), this cannot be true of all. A critical response to such an argument would be as follows. What is really meant by the classificatory sense of art? Do we use this sense in our everyday talk about art? Why should we regard anything as art if we do not attach any "value" to it, whatever that be? The point of our argument is that only when we come across something which we take to be valuable in some respect that we use the term art. Use of the term art is done only when we *regard* something as *valuable*. This indeed is its core sense; any other sense would only be peripheral. The "two senses" theory would thus stand debunked.

Third, analytic approach to aesthetic discourse shows a great deal of preoccupation with art, *not* as much with *natural beauty*. How can we avoid or ignore philosophical reflection on our response to beauty in nature? To put the matter in perspective, our earliest promptings of aesthetical thinking spring forth from the delight we derive from our response to nature. We experience beauty first and foremost in nature and then in artefacts. How can we relegate this original sense of beauty and reflection on it into the background? And by doing so, the larger philosophical issues concerning the relation between art and nature of life do not receive the kind of attention that it deserves in any aesthetical discourse. Among all the analytic aestheticians, M.C. Beardsley alone perhaps carried out a detailed analysis of aesthetic experience. Many among these thinkers have gone on to even debunk the concept of aesthetic experience. For instance, G. Dickie maintains that driving through a crowded street is qualitatively no different from what is claimed as aesthetic experience.

Fourth, the analytic aesthetician's concerns have remained focused on the nature of the finished product or the artefact and the locutions about it. By developing the idea of analysing such locutions, M.C. Beardsley opens out an interesting trend, aesthetics as *metacriticism*. This involves taking apart the different kinds of statements about art into, descriptive, interpretative, and evaluative statements and going into the logic of their language. For Beardsley, these three different types of statement provide the hunting ground for philosophical aesthetics. But it might be said by way rejoinder here that the domain of philosophical aesthetics is much wider than that of metacriticism.

And finally, analytic aesthetics shows a bias against treating art objects as value-laden objects. Value judgments which are based on the special delight or satisfaction that the works of art may provide remain suspect to the philosopher of analytic persuasion. It is in this context that we may understand the significance of the attempts of some philosophers (Rowe, Hanfling et al.) to define art in terms of its *function*.

To conclude, we would say that analytic aesthetics has shown an overarching concern with the analysis and clarification of concepts. This task indeed has its merits which hardly needs stressing. However, such an approach also carries limitations. Given all its merits, analytic aesthetics remains sterile in the matter of providing new insights and visions which would follow a more comprehensive and synoptic approach to questions relating to art and its relation to life and society. Questions concerning aesthetic experience, ineffability of aesthetic emotions, standards of greatness in art and many other issues related thereto do not receive any serious attention.

References

Beardsley, M. C. (1978). The aesthetic point of view. In J. Margolis (Ed.), *Philosophy looks at the arts*. Philadelphia: Temple University Press.

Dickie, G. (1971). *Aesthetics: An introduction*. New York: Bobbs-Merrill.

Gallie, W. B. (1956). Art as an essentially contested concept. *The Philosophical Quarterly, 6*, 97–114.

Hampshire, S. (1970 Reprint). Logic and appreciation. In W. Elton (Ed.), *Aesthetics and language* (pp. 161–169). Oxford: Blackwell.

Hanfling, O. (1995, January). Art, artifacts and function. *Philosophical Investigation, 18*, 1.

Hermeren, G. (1995, June). Art and life: Models for understanding music. *The Australasian Journal of Philosophy, 73*(2).

Kennick, W. E. (1958). Does traditional aesthetics rest on a mistake? *Mind, 67*, 317–334.

Langer, S. K. (1953). *Feeling and form*. New York: Routledge and Kegan Paul.

Lord, C. (1987). Indexicality, not circularity: Dickie's new definition of art. *The Journal of Aesthetics andArt Criticism, XIV*(3), 229–232.

Mandelbaum, M. (1979). Family resemblances and generalizations concerning the arts. In M. Rader (Ed.), *A modern book of esthetics* (5th ed.). Rinehart and Winston: Holt.

Margolis, J. (1980). *Art and philosophy: Conceptual issues in esthetics*. USA: Humanities Press.

McDonald, M. (1965). Some distinctive features of arguments used in criticism of the arts. In J. Stolnitz (Ed.), *Aesthetics* (pp. 98–112). New York: Macmillan.

Mothersill, M. (1967, August). 'Unique' as an aesthetic predicate. *The Journal of Philosophy, LVIII*(16), 393–437.

Rowe, M. W. (1991, July). Why art doesn't have two senses? *The British Journal of Aesthetics, 31*(3), 217–219.

Shusterman, R. (1989). *Analytic aesthetics*. Oxford: Basil Blackwell.

Tilghman, B. R. (1984). *But is it art?* Oxford: Blackwell.

Weitz, M. (1956). The role of theory in aesthetics. *The Journal of Aesthetics and Art Criticiism, 15*, 27–35.

Chapter 2
The Literary Text: Meaning and Intention

Abstract It deals with the basic question relating to the role of intention in understanding the meaning of a literary text. The term "intention" in the context of the literary text is problematic as it has been understood in various senses such as that of the historical author or poet, that which is objectified in the text or that which is bestowed upon it by the reader. The chapter begins with the epoch making paper on "intentional fallacy" by Wimsatt Jr. and Beardsley and New Criticism and goes on to the various subsequent developments in this direction till we reach the trends in post-structuralism and postmodernism. It is argued that understanding the literary meaning of a poem or text is not quite the same as apprehending the poetic or creative meaning.

Keywords Intentionalism · Anti-intentionalism · New Criticism · Speech act theory · Poetic meaning · Post-stucturalism

What is the meaning of a poem? Can it have a meaning other than what is claimed as the poet's intention? Such questions are raised in the context of a literary text. Meaning of a literary text is often worked out quite independently of the authorial intention. The identification of the literary meaning (or interpretation) with authorial intention has met with sharp objections thanks to the *New Criticism* and its doctrinal position of "the intentional fallacy" as argued by Wimsatt Jr. and Beardsley.[1] It derecognizes any privileged access to the literary text that is claimed by the author. In the main, the criticism against intentionalism rests if the contention that the objective meaning can be available by a close reading of the text itself, the meaning intended must be suspended in the event of any objective means to get it.

---

[1] Wimsatt and Beardsley (1946), since reprinted in many anthologies. The basic argument put forward is that either the text contains the poet's intention or it does not. If it does, then the text is where we should be looking for it, if not, then it is not relevant at all. So we commit a fallacy by looking for the intention of the author in the mind of the author or the alleged presence of it there. Only a closer reading of the text will suffice to accomplish this task. Also, for detailed analyses of the concept of intention in art, see Ghosh (1987a, b).

However, the concept of intention has remained alive. Intentionalism is based on the argument that there can be no meaning without the intention of the author (Ghosh 1987c). We may distinguish here, broadly speaking, two senses in which the concept of intention may be understood in the context of the literary text. There is indeed a *general* sense in which all such works are *intentionally* made rather than made by chance or accident. This applies to all cases of art including literary arts, visual arts and performing arts and so on. Thus a work of art must be regarded as the product of conscious and deliberate human endeavour. This general sense of intention is unexceptionable and cannot be contested on any account.

There is, however, a more *specific* sense of the term "intention" in which it is identified with the *meaning* (or the aesthetic context) of a work of art. And it is *this* sense that has been argued for by Steven Knapp and Walter Michael (1982). According to them, the *meaning* of a poem is to be identified with the poet's intention. If intention is taken as the criterion of meaningfulness in the *earlier* sense, here it is its very *meaning*. It is important to understand the implications of the view. In the first place, such a view is directed *not* against the anti-intentionalism of Wimsatt and Beardsley (New Criticism) (Wimsatt and Beardsley 1946). The latter only holds that the meaning of the text is *embodied* in it and does not require us to look for it outside of it, say, in the mind of the anther. Indeed, the author's intention is only implanted in the text, if it is successfully carried out by him. So why look into the mind of the author? Further if it is not successfully carried out by the author, then there is all the more reason not to bother about it. In other words, such a view only suggests the methodology by which to establish the embodied meaning of the text. Their only objection is the use of the term intention which is a mentalistic term; meaning is regarded as what is objectively understood.

But the position taken by Knapp and Michael is against the post-structuralist for whom the meaning of the literary text is what the reader makes of it. The post-structuralists (Paul de Man and many others) see the literary text as intentionless language rather than intentional speech acts. They argue that it is the reader that bestows meaning on the text, and thus every reader is free to read into it *any* meaning. Such a position leads to meaning *pluralism*. According to Knapp and Michael, the meaning of the text is the intention of the author. Interestingly, anti-intentionalism can be looked at in two ways. Wimsatt and Beardsley argue against the notion of authorial intention because, for them, the text *embodies* its meaning that the reader may discover by giving it close reading. Their *objection* is only to the use of the mentalistic term "intention" since the meaning is discoverable objectively. To look for this meaning into the *mind* of the author is to commit the "intentional fallacy". In short, the meaning is the text, not in the mind of the author.

The anti-intentionalism of the kind that is associated with the post-structuralist thinkers precisely *disagrees* with the first part of the statement above though it *agrees* with the latter part of it. The agreement is on the point that the meaning of the text is not the claim about the supposed authorial intention. However they *disagree* that the meaning is *not* in the text either. One could speak of a *plurality* of meanings according as each reader is able to make sense of the text. As Terry

Eagleton[2] says, the meaning is "produced" by the text, it is not "expressed" or "reflected" in language. Further, meaning is produced "differently" for different readers depending on the form of social life one belongs to. According to this view, meaning is what the *reader* makes of it from the text.

So when Wimsatt and Beardsley attack intentionalism of the nineteenth century theorists, they share with them the assumption that the literary text could have only one *single correct* meaning or interpretation.[3] The only divergence is with regard to the point as to where to look for it, in the *mind* of the author or in the *text?* But the anti-intentionalism of the post-structuralist strain debunks the very idea of the text having only one single meaning. On this view, the text may admit of *multiple* meanings depending on the ability of the reader. Here, the author stands totally marginalized.

Before we go back to the anti-intentionalism of Knapp and Michael, let us look at the anti-intentionalism of Wimsatt and Beardsley from another perspective. They are indeed opposed to the identification of the meaning of the literary text with the meaning that is said to be intended by the *author*. But we may draw here a distinction between the author's intended meaning (or the authorial intention) and the intention implicit in the speech act of the *speaker* internal to the text. The literary text may be regarded as the speech act made by the supposed internal speaker of the text. This claim is made on the ground that only language as *speech* act may lay claim to meaningfulness. Speech act is, indeed, *intentional* in character. It goes without saying that the search for such speaker's intention must consist in looking closely at the text itself. Thus Wimsatt and Beardsley claim that their engagement is with the search for the *objective* meaning of the text. Their anti-intentionalism does not renege against the talk about the speaker's intention being identical to the objective meaning of the text. William Dowling (1985) sums up by pointing out that the distinction between author and speaker warranted close reading of the text as a formalist or New Critical mode of interpretation. Ignoring the empirical author does not entail ignoring the *speaker* who actually narrates in the text. In this context, the question that one may ask is, can there be language in the *absence* of a speaker's intention?

For the anti-intentionalism of Knapp and Michael (1982), the alleged distinction between meaning and intention collapses. According to them, intentionless language is a contradiction in terms. They hold the view that intentionalism is not a matter of choice, nor does intention provide a theory or method of interpreting a

---

[2] Eagleton calls it "paradigm shift", "Indeed one might very roughly periodize the history of modern literary theory in three stages: a preoccupation with the author (Romanticism and the nineteenth century; an exclusive concern with the text (Criticism), and a marked shift of attention to the reader over recent years." Eagleton (1995, 74).

[3] Please see Richard Shusterman, as he says "Their defense of intentionalism is not directed against Beardsley and Wimsatt (whose New Critical program has already been superseded by more recent and fashionable theories) but primarily at today's prevailing a anti intentionalists—the post-structuralists like de Man—who see literary texts as *intentionless* language rather than intended speech acts, which instead are what Knapp and Michael maintain all language must always be" in Shusterman (1988, emphasis added).

text. Intention always plays a role in language, and meaning and intention are identical to each other. Making sense of a text is doing so in terms of intention. Further, they hold the view that interpretation of literary text does not require any theory.

The alleged dichotomy between the poem's meaning and the poet's meaning arises on the assumption that, since the poet's intention not being directly accessible, it is possible to fall back on the meaning that accretes directly from the words or sentences in the poem. In a recent paper, John Searle (1994) has claimed that the distinction between sentence meaning and speaker meaning is relevant to our understanding of the meaning of a *literary* text. He joins issue with Knapp and Michael by *maintaining* the distinction between meaning and intention. In support of this distinction, Searle points to the example of the "wave poem", the imaginary case of coming upon a few lines from a Wordsworth poem that are found scribbled on the beach after the sea waves recede. He argues that even if these lines had been made by the sea waves, it is possible to get at the sentence meaning on the basis of the syntactical structure of the lines. Thus on Searle's view, the *conventional meaning* of these accidentally made sentences has an independent status, and this should not be confused with the *speaker meaning*. This is a rejoinder to the view held by Knapp and Michael (intentionalism) that meaning and intention are identical and a distinction between the two is unwarranted.

The main thrust of Searle's[4] argument is this. What makes language or sentences meaningful is the condition of satisfiability of the conventional rules of grammar and syntax even if such occurrence happens by chance (as in the case of "wave poem"). Meaningfulness of language is a function of rule satisfiability of grammar and syntax. For example, fiddling with the computer keyboard by a pet cat may produce by sheer chance a perfect English sentence, say, "The chair is made of wood". Indeed, one can multiply such examples. (a) Imagine a young student who is learning a foreign language by the district method. Now when this person utters aloud after her teacher the sentence "This building is on fire!", another person who knows the language passes the room and panics on hearing the utterance. Interestingly, neither the teacher nor the student ever *intended* to say what the utterance *means*. Clearly in such cases sentence *meaning* may function independently of *speaker* meaning. When the student utters the sentence she understands its conventional meaning without adding her *intention* to it. Searle stresses the points (i) that a distinction between sentence meaning and speaker meaning is quite in order and (ii) that sentence meaning could accrue even where it is not intended by the speaker. In fairness to Searle, the point at (ii) should not be misconstrued to mean that there *actually* exists an authorless language. His claim about the distinction between *sentence* meaning (conventional or literal meaning) and *intended* meaning is well established by such illustrations. One might argue, though, that there is perhaps a derivative sense in which marks produced of utterance made by sheer chance are considered meaningful because they resemble the sentences with conscious intention. However, the central point in Searle's argument is that sentence meaning is

---

[4] For a detailed discussion, please see Ghosh (1997).

distinguishable from speaker meaning. Now to our mind, the distinction seems valid only in the context of our everyday language though Searle claims it for the *literary* text as well.

By way of a rejoinder to Searle, we would argue that this transition from what goes on in everyday language to the domain of poetic meaning is quite unwarranted. For, Searle merely assumes what he is required to establish, that is, that the literary text is no different from our everyday language. The Searlean distinction between sentence meaning and speaker meaning is quite unacceptable to Knapp and Michael (1985). For them, meaning and intention are inseparable. In their view, the object of all reading is always the historical author's intention. In their "Reply to Searle", they hold that "the distinction between sentence meaning and speaker meaning is *real* but is not (as Searle Calls it) a distinction between 'two kinds of meaning'; it is instead a distinction between two ways of meaning, by following the rules and by not following them, and these two ways are equally intentional" (Knapp and Michael 1994, 674).

The following two points may be made here. First, how do they hope to find the meaning "by not following" the rules? Second, if by "two ways of meaning" they suggest that the *same* meaning may be arrived at by following two different ways, then this should be applicable, on this view, to both everyday language and the literary text. But, on our view, what is crucial to the debate is the very distinctive nature of the literary text. How do we account for the distinction between everyday language and the literary text?

Whenever we use language as a discursive means, the notion of sentence meaning is operative. Also we are sometime aware of the gap between sentence meaning and speaker meaning in our everyday communication. At times, there is a deliberate attempt or intention to create or maintain this gap; this is often the case with political statements. The notion of sentence meaning has only a peripheral role, that of providing the criterion for identifying something as a sentence token. The hearer, on the other hand, aims at finding out the specific speaker meaning. But on what grounds do we distinguish the literary text (poetic language) from everyday language? Here the notion of sentence meaning has no relevance whatsoever. Take, for example, the road sign "NO PARKING". We understand the meaning without verifying whether it was put there by the sign painter for the paint to dry up or whether it was deliberately put up to regulate the traffic. The meaning of the road sign is clear without any consideration of the intention for it to be there. Perhaps this is what Searle wants to argue for by distinguishing sentence meaning from speaker meaning.

As against this view of Searle, Knapp and Michael hold the view that language, in any circumstance, consists of intentional speech acts.[5] They seem to think that by stressing this point they could debunk Searle's argument in favour of sentence meaning. On our view, the attack is misdirected as they fail to see the real weakness

---

[5] In their "Reply to Our Critics": "What can the word 'author' mean if not the composer of the text? In our view to postulate' an author is already to commit oneself to an account of the composer of the text, and there is nothing to choose between them *because they are the same*" (Knapp and Michael 1985, 101, emphasis added).

in Searlean position. We would point out a real chink in his standpoint. It is this that Searle does not draw a distinction or takes note of it between the *literary text* and everyday language. How does one know whether or not something (any textual matter) is *intended* to be a *literary* text? The author or poet makes such an intention apparent by publishing it or by presenting it to the audience in a certain contextual situation. The act of publishing, displaying in public, presenting to the audience, etc. is quite comparable to making a speech act. One puts forward a claim for it to be regarded as a work of art, say, a painting, poem, novel etc. The examples of driftwood art or the "Dada" propensity to bestow the title of art on "found" or castaway objects clearly illustrate the point.[6] So our argument with regard to Searle's example of "wave poem" would be as follows. Unless the "wave marks" are claimed by someone as *intended* to be regarded as a poem, they would only remain as wave marks and not as poem. The role of intention is crucial to our appreciation of a work of art. Art objects are not products of chance or accident; they are made intentionally.

So the important question to ask here is: Are the marks on the beach a poem? Or, would Searle claim the marks to be a poem because the marks satisfy the rules of grammar and syntax? But if that were the case, then anyone could claim to write a poem just by uttering some words that would satisfy the conventional rules of grammar and syntax. Crucial to our understanding, the point here is that a poem is identified as one not merely because it satisfies the conventional rules of grammar and syntax (sometimes it does not do even that very strictly) as it transcends such conditionality. According to Knapp and Michael, intentionalism is not a matter of choice, nor does it provide a theory or method of interpreting a text. Rather, it always plays a role in language such that it is not for anyone either to leave it or take it while talking about the meaning of a text. Meaning and intention are identical to each other. Thus interpretation of the literary text does not require any theory.

It is possible to understand the discussion in terms of the following points: (a) we may interpret the literary text in terms of its intention, or (b) we may interpret the literary text in terms of the intention of its author. In (a) "its intention" stands for the intention of an author, that is to say, that it refers to an author that is posited as internal to the text. But in (b) "the intention of its author" would refer to the historical or empirical author's real intention. As we have pointed out earlier, Wimsatt and Beardsley object to (b) but have no quarrel with (a). According to them, (a) is available objectively by" close reading" of the text itself.

However, Knapp and Michael are not prepared to grant a separation between (a) and (b), and thus conflate the two.[7] Their intentionalism critiques on the one hand

---

[6] For a detailed discussion on Duchamp's *Fountain* (an instance of Dada art), see Goldsmith (1983, 197–208); as also for a related context, see Ghosh (1989).

[7] For Knapp and Michael, meaning and intention are inseparable. In their reply to Searle, they hold that "the distinction between sentence meaning and speaker meaning is *real* but is not (as Searle calls it) a distinction between 'two kinds of meaning'; it is instead a distinction between two ways of meaning, by following the rules and by not following them, and these two ways are equally intentional" (Knapp and Michael, n.d., 674).

the anti-intentionalism of the sort that is advocated by post-structuralist thinkers while on the other hand also dissociating itself from the position of these thinkers (E.D. Hirsh and P.D. Juhl) who regard intentionalism as a methodological requirement for the interpretation of the literary text.

Now, in order to have a better understanding about the concept of intention, we may raise the following questions: (i) What is the nature of such intention? (ii) Is it given in the poet's mind prior to undertaking the creative process? (iii) How do we have knowledge of such intention? (v) How is such knowledge verifiable? The first two questions have a bearing on the ontological status of the creative work such as whether it is to be identified with the mental process. The other two questions are connected to epistemological issues. Turning to some of these matters, we way note that the creative process remains somewhat shrouded in mystery. Moreover, each individual artist is given to practices that may not be the same for the others. The criterion of prior planning may not be useful for arriving at a view about the authorial intention. Also, the notion of prior planning may be applicable to certain forms of art such as architecture, film-making for which the process requires detailed planning in advance. This may not be true of say a poem or a hurriedly executed drawing. So, a narrow and rigid sense of intention cannot be invoked for addressing the questions at (i) and (ii) above. We would do well also to distinguish the various senses of intentions in terms of "prior" intention, "original" intention, "subsequent" intention and "later" intention. If intention is to be understood as a fixed idea or plan in the mind of the artist, then perhaps such an approach would seem to be quite relevant. But from the standpoint of the viewer/reader, it is only the actualized intention that crucially matters for the appreciation and interpretation of the work. One is not necessarily to deal with certain alleged mental states or events while referring to the artist's intention.

Here, it would be useful to draw a distinction between intentions in the context of our everyday life activities on one hand and artist's intentions, on the other. In the context of everyday life, while making a statement about something, the speaker would be quite clear of his intention and yet may want to camouflage the same by making an utterance that conveys something else. This is often the case with people in politics or public life. When caught on the wrong foot on some issue, there is always an attempt to get out of such a situation by claiming that it was not really intended. But the cases of artist's intention are more complex in nature as they relate to (a) the *medium* and the way it is manipulated, (b) the semantic structure that is woven into it and (c) the aesthetic appearance that is given to the work. The artist may be vaguely aware of some of these but can claim no prior knowledge about them. In other words, most of these intentions are not sayable. How the medium is handled and what structure the work finally gets to assume are things that no poet or artist can visualize by way of prior knowledge or planning. Very often it is the case that the medium begins to prompt the artist as to the next word or stroke in the work. Yet the work would be regarded as a product of conscious intention. The point we are trying to make is that artistic intention, being non-propositional in nature, often remains unclear even to the artist/author. For example, bursting forth of a string of words carries along the poet in a way that defies any conscious and statable planning or intention. Relationship between words in a poem occurs quite independently of any conscious plan on the mind of the poet. So Tagore puts it so eloquently, it is the "tide of creation" (Neogi 1961) that carries the artist/poet along the path of creative destination. There may be promptings to the poet from some unknowable source which might be clear to him after the poem is composed (For a fuller discussion on this see Ghosh 2006). The aesthetic significance of such intentions can be apprehended only within the total structure and context of the creative work.

The irony underlying the position taken by Knapp and Michael is that their formulation of the intentionality thesis does not warrant any talk about the artist's intention as it is always identical with what is taken to be the meaning of the text. Such a position, in a way, comes close to the stand taken by Wimsatt Jr. and Beardsley when they argue that no reference need be made to the intention of the author or else it would be committing a fallacy. From the point of view of critical practice, there is hardly any difference between the two positions.

We would argue that even if we concede the Searlean thesis about rule satisfiability and meaningfulness of sentence meaning, these would not help us decide whether something is a poem. White arguing about the determining criterion for sentence tokens, Searle has leapfrogged to the domain of the literary text without any logical warrant. Significantly, this seems to have escaped the notice of the opponents. Searle argues that a set of marks would be language (sentence tokens) if they satisfy the rules of grammar and syntax. On the other hand, Knapp and Michael would want to defend their thesis that the meaning of a poem must be identified with the poet's intention as there is no other meaning available. In other words, the very identity of a literary text is to be understood in terms of the intended meaning. Searle does not advance any argument against this position. Whatever is said by him about the distinction between sentence meaning and speaker meaning is in the context of sentence tokens only.

Now, to our mind, the central point on which Searle and his opponents should really focus their attention on may be outlined here. Is the identity of a poem reducible to sentence tokens? If so, then the implications would be as follows: (1) A poem is composed only of sentence tokens. (2) Sentence tokens do not require, as shown in the "wave poem" example, any intending act for their production. (3) Their meaning is also reducible to some other sentence tokens. If (1) is accepted then anything might be claimed as a poem. And, if (2) and (3) are accepted, then there can be no such thing as poetic meaning.

Searle seems to be arguing that no actual act of intending is necessary for a set of marks, caused by the receding waves on the shore, to be treated as language. But Knapp and Michael need not join issue with him on this point. Rather, they should object to this being conflated with the determining criteria for the literary text. While Searle wants to dispense with the requirement of an actual act of intending for the possibility of rule satisfiability in the case of ordinary or common use of language, this does not help him to come to grips with the way that literary texts are produced. Searle speaks of the "intentionality of the system" for the rule-governed nature of language instead of an actual act of intending.

We would want to respond to this in the following way. In the case of the literary text (say, a poem), departure from the rules of grammar and syntax may bring into play a new range of meanings. But the knowledge of an intending act to do so is of the essence of any appreciation of the value so created. To put the matter differently, violation of the rules of grammar and syntax may sometimes heighten specific emotive content. On Searle's argument such waywardness would not count for sentence tokens. Nor can such instances claim to have sentence meaning either. But he fails to see that a sympathetic reader should at once see the intention of the poet and the significance of the deviant lines in the poem. We hold the view that poetic meaning cannot be grasped independently of the poet's intention.

Further, the dichotomy between sentence meaning and speaker meaning may arise in the context of our everyday language. But the critic who deals with the poetic language is concerned only with what the poet expresses in and through the poem. The two main difficulties with the Searlean position may be outlined as follows. First, a poem is not merely the sum total of conventional sentences, and hence the notion of sentence meaning would be unworkable here. Second, he fails to take note of the distinction between ordinary language and poetic language. If something qualifies to be language on the principle of rule satisfiability, it would not follow from this that it could be regarded as a poem on the basis of the criterion of rule satisfiability. Our concern here is to be able to decide whether something is a poem and not a limerick, a painting and not a poster, a short story and not a newspaper report, a sculpture and not a block of stone and so on. We would argue that the artist's intention plays an important role in helping us to come to a decision in such matters. Works of art are not products of chance, and so they cannot be delinked from the processes that make it possible for them to come into existence.

The paradoxical nature of creativity baffles even the artist while he remains a conscious participant in the whole process. True, the poem that is composed by the poet is not merely a matter of chance. But he cannot formulate the rule by which it was created. So our enquiry does not merely relate to whether or not something is language (as is the case with Searle) but rather to the question whether or not something is poetic language. So Searle fails to come to grips with this creative situation on the basis of his distinction between sentence meaning and speaker meaning. There are rules by the use of and reference to which we can make meaningful sentences and make sense for what others utter. But there are no such rules and criteria by which we can make, say, poems? There are intentions that one apprehends while reading a poem, though these are not paraphrasable without loss of their real import.

In conclusion, we would say that the distinction between language and literary text as a creative product is crucial to our understanding of intentionalism in the context of the literary text. Understanding the literal meaning is not quite the same as apprehending the poetic meaning. Rule satisfiability may provide the criteria for sentence meaning, but there are no specific rules for making poems. In literary arts as much as in all other arts, meaning cannot be abstracted away from the way (or form) in which it arises in the particular work of art. It is the non-propositional (nondiscursive) import that is claimed as the distinctive meaning of the creative work. For that matter, non-propositional intentions are directly felt or experienced since these are not sayable emitters. It is for this reason that Searle's notion of sentence meaning would not fit in with the unsayable intentions that one directly confronts and feels in a poem. In literary arts as much as in all other arts, meaning cannot be abstracted away from the way (or form) in which it arises in the particular work of art. It is the non-propositional (nondiscursive) import that is claimed as the distinctive meaning of the creative work. For that matter, non-propositional intentions are directly felt or experienced since these are not sayable entities. It is for these reasons that Searle's notion of sentence meaning would not fit in with the unsayable intentions that one directly confronts and feels in a poem. The core content of a poem or any literary text is an object of direct experience.

References

Dowling, W. C. (1985). Intentionless meaning. In W. J. T. Mitchell (Ed.), *Against theory: Literary studies and the new pragmatism*. Chicago: University of Chicago Press.

Eagleton, T. (1995). *Literary theory: An introduction*. Oxford: Blackwell.

Ghosh, R. K. (1987a). The logic of our talk about the Artist's intention. *Indian Philosophical Quarterly, XIV*(3).

Ghosh, R. K. (1987b). *Concepts and presuppositions in aesthetics*. Delhi: Ajanta Publications Chapter: "The Concept of Intention".

Ghosh, R. K. (1987c). The logic of our talk about the artist's intention. *Indian Philosophical Quarterly, Vol XIV No, 3*.

Ghosh, R. K. (1989). Art domesticity, aesthetic significance. In J. James (Ed.), *Art and life in India 'The last four decades'*. Shimla: IIAS.

Ghosh, R. K. (2006). *Great Indian thinkers on art: Creativity, aesthetic communication, and freedom*. Delhi: Black and White (An Imprint of Sundeep Prakashan).

Ghosh, R. K. (1997, January–April). Sentence meaning, intentionalism, and the literary text: An interface. *Journals of Indian Council of Philosophical Research, XIV*(2).

Goldsmith, S. (1983, Winter). The Readymades of Marcel Duchamp: the ambiguities of an aesthetic revolution. *The Journal of Aesthetics and Art Criticism*.

Knapp, S., & Michael, W. (1982, Summer). Against theory. *Critical Inquiry*, (8), 723–742.

Knapp, S., & Michael, W. (1985). Reply to our critics. In W. T. J. Mitchell (Ed.), *Against theory: Literary studies and the new pragmatism*. Chicago: University of Chicago Press.

Knapp, S., & Michael, W. (1994, Summer). Reply to searle. *New Literary History, 25*, 674.

Neogi, P. (Ed.). (1961). *Rabindranath Tagore on art and aesthetics: From a selection of lectures, essays and letters*. Calcutta: Orient Longmans.

Searle, J. R. (1994, Summer). Literary theory and its discontent. *New Literary History, 25* (Henceforth NLH).

Shusterman, R. (1988, Spring). Interpretation, intention, and truth. *The Journal of Aesthetics and Art Criticism*.

Wimsatt, W. K., Jr., & Beardsley, M. C. (1946). The intentional fallacy. *Sewanee Review, LIV*, 3–23.

Chapter 3
Emotions in Art

Abstract The chapter mainly deals with the questions about the ontological status of emotions that we *experience for a character or incident, say, a novel, movie,* etc. *Is the experience we have of,* say, anger, pity, sympathy, etc., in relation to the characters in a novel, poem, play, etc. real and rational? Or, is it the case that these are "make-belief" and "irrational?" This also brings in its wake the question about relation between literature and truth. It is important to understand that the feelings experienced in the context of a literary work are experienced without their attendant consequences and the anticipated reactions thereto. These feelings are savoured without being affected by their attendant consequences. By way of understanding the nature of such emotions, a distinction is being suggested between "pretending to oneself" and "pretending to others". The argument has been developed that in creative works it is the case of "pretending to oneself".

Keywords Make-belief emotions · Irrational emotions · Pretence · Pretending to *oneself*

It is indeed interesting to understand the nature of emotions that are often felt in relation to certain characters or incidents in a novel or poem. Are these emotions real or make-believe? For example, when we feel pity for a character in a novel, is it the same kind of emotion that we experience in real life? When we feel pity for a person in real life, such a person is also real. But the person in the novel is a fictional character. In real-life situations, the person we feel pity for is not a fictional character.

In recent years, Christopher New (1999, p. 53) raises question about the ontological status of emotions that we experience for a character or incident in a novel, movie, etc. He points out that when the reaction of fear (or any other emotion such as anger, pity, sympathy, etc.) arises in response to a work of art, we do not believe that such a response is to a real being. On the other hand, our feeling of an emotion towards a person or situation in real life is accompanied by the belief that it is for a real person.

To put the matter a little more in concrete terms, when the reaction of fear arises in the mind in response to some incident or character in a novel, we do not believe

© The Author(s), under exclusive license to Springer Nature Singapore Pte Ltd. 2018   23
R. K. Ghosh, *Essays in Literary Aesthetics*, SpringerBriefs in Philosophy,
https://doi.org/10.1007/978-981-13-2460-4_3

that our response is to a real being or incident. Nor is our behavioural disposition accompanied by an impulse to escape the occurrence though we may experience quickened pulse rate, sweating palms, etc. Christopher New argues that in such cases how can we claim to really be experiencing fear?[1]

Two important questions arise: (1) Are such responses only "make-believe?" (2) If the responses are real, are they "irrational"? Kendall Walton[2] answers (i) in the affirmative. He cites the example in which a child is playing the game of "make-belief" with his father who pretends to be a monster. The child knows that it is a case of "make-belief" world because there is no real monster. In the same way, art situations (drama, novel, etc.) are also "make-believe", and while responding to them, we know that we are actually confronted with a make-believe world just as the child knows that it is only a "game".

There is, however, a serious difficulty with this kind of an approach. It is true that such negative emotions (fear, pity, etc.) when felt in response to a work of fiction are not accompanied by any behavioural changes, e.g. calling for help. But one does feel bodily sensations like faster pulse rate, horripilation, etc. much as they do happen in real-life situations. So the theory that our psychological responses to a work are make-believe cannot explain why one experiences the sensations and other bodily changes. Also remains unexplained the fact that after we have put away the novel, we describe our psychological reactions in the same way as we do in real-life situations. Does it follow that we are merely pretending to ourselves that we feel this or that emotion merely in a make-believe world? But consider for a moment the comic emotions. Our laughter here is real; we do not pretend to ourselves that we are laughing. Thus the thesis of "make-believe" reaction is open to several points of criticism. Alex Neil[3] points out some of these points and argues that Walton fails to satisfy this requirement that lacks the explanatory value.

We may now turn to the view at (2) whereby it is argued that these emotions are "irrational". According to this view, our reaction of fear, pity, etc. are real though these are directed to what is only fictional and not real. Is it the case that we forget that the characters are fictional and lake them for real? But, this cannot happen all

---

[1] "How then can I really be experiencing fear? Or if, alternately, I really am experiencing fear, must I not either have forgotten that nothing dangerous is really happening to any real person, in which case I am childishly deluded, or else simply be afraid where there is no cause for fear, in which case I am childishly irrational." (New 1999, pp. 53–4).

[2] Walton takes a position when he compares it to a situation in which a child is playing "a game of make-believe" with his father who is *pretending* to be a monster. The child screams and runs, but he knows that it is only a "game". So he remarks thus: "When the slime raised the head, spies the camera, and begins oozing towards it, it is make-believe that Charles is threatened…. Charles is playing a game of make-believe in which he uses the images on the screen as a prop." (Walton 1978, p. 13).

[3] "Just as an analysis of the concept of fear must, if it is to have real explanatory value, allows to distinguish fear from other emotions, so on account of what constitutes make-believably fearing something must allow us to say what distinguishes that state from others such as being make-believably anxious or angry or upset. I shall argue that Walton's account fails to satisfy this requirement, and that it lacks the explanatory value that would warrant, its acceptance." (Neil 1991, pp. 52–3).

the time with all the readers. Surely, most readers are not deluded to take fictional characters and events as real.[4] So, some theorists claim that they are irrational. For example, the film *Titanic* evokes intense emotional response. It is ostensibly an exploration into a past event, a technique by which the story of the film is distanced away from the audience. We are aware that the event is not happening now. Yet all our psychological responses such as fear, suspense and pity are all directed to the film as if these responses were in the context of what we are watching now. This phenomenon calls for further analysis. Let us proceed as follows.

In the first place, psychological reactions when experienced in the context of real-life situations are accompanied by suitable commensurate behavioural changes. But in the context of a film or novel, our responses are unaccompanied by such baggage. Second, our psychological responses in the context of a film or novel are accompanied by a belief in the fictional nature of the presented or enacted event. In real life though, such responses arise on the ground of the belief that the situation and characters are not fictional. Here one would want to avoid situations that cause any negative emotions. While in the context of a film or novel, our responses are always accompanied by a sense of satisfaction or relish, and even negative emotions such as pity and fear are enjoyed. Third, our experience of emotions in life is often followed by a decision to vent them out in one way or the other. But, emotions experienced in art are not only relished but are of a kind that the others are also invited to participate in and share with. Fourth, it is also necessary to draw a distinction between what merely arouses bestial passions on one hand and what becomes an object of experience on the other. So experiencing emotions in the context of art is on a reflective plane if it happens to a good work of art. Fifth, one experiences an emotional state in life as an individuated event. But in the context of a novel or film, the emotions are felt as part of an organic whole. These various emotions are not unconnected to each other and make sense only in the context of the whole. Lastly, it follows that since our psychological responses are in relation to a work of art that embodies finality, such reactions are shorn of any reactive manoeuvres that would affect our behaviour as a whole. Here we are quite conscious of the fictionality of the work unlike it is the case in real life.

In the final analysis, one might raise the following question here. If one is consciously aware that, say, Anna Karenina is a fictional character, how do we come to feel pity for her? In another example, say, the film, *Titanic*, we feel a strong sense of pity for the young lover even when we are fully aware that it is a work of fiction. The argument cannot be that we forget that it is fictional. Yet, we feel pity or some such psychological reaction in its context. Obviously, we cannot describe it as "irrational". How do we go about this problem?

We would want to draw here a distinction between pretence and fiction. Pretence presupposes that the act be taken as real though it is a fake in reality. e.g. the talk

---

[4]Peter McCormick holds the view that "we are not moved by something we know does not exist. What genuinely moves us, rather, are our actual thoughts about something that does not exist. The objects of our feelings are not beliefs but thought-contents. We respond emotionally, then, to thought-contest and not to beliefs at all" (McCormick 1988, p. 137).

about fake beggar can be understood in relation to a real beggar. When we come to somehow know that the person is only pretending to be a beggar, our earlier emotion of pity towards him will disappear and may even be replaced by anger, irritation and so on. But this is not so in the case of fiction or "make-believe". Novels and films, for example, are based on fiction, and yet it is quite natural to feel pity or anger towards a character.

In the case of a work of fiction, we can meaningfully talk about pretence or make-believe. Take, for example, the case of a detective fiction in which the real culprit remains unsuspected till about the end of the story when the mystery is solved. All through the story, the unsuspecting culprit might even evoke in the reader some tender feelings towards him that suddenly disappear when the culprit stands exposed at the end. Now we can here talk about the pretence of the real culprit. But what do we mean by "real" culprit since it is a work of fiction? It makes sense to do so because the work of fiction is our only universe of discourse. In spite of our implicit awareness about its functionality, we refer to the character as real culprit.

Somewhat similar would be the case for a cricket or football match between rival teams in which the spectator may naturally support one of them and has pro-feelings for it. The psychological reactions against the other team may be so strong and intense even though it is only a game and not a real war. Our point here is that regardless of even being a situation of real war or just one of make-believe (i.e. game), the psychological reactions cannot be termed as make-believe; they are real emotions.

We may now turn to the architecture of the usage of the term "pretence". We would distinguish between *witnessing* others to pretend to others from pretending to one's own self. Now what does it mean to pretend to oneself? Let us take an example. If an artist has to act out a character, it can be done either by merely pretending to others or by pretending to oneself the identity of the character in the film or drama. And this would mean that while enacting the role, the artist has to feel as if he was actually himself that character undergoing all its emotion. In such a case, the gap between the identity of the actor and that of the role performed will end to be non-existent. Interestingly mimicry artists make the gap between the two identities deliberately visible in order to evoke comic reactions in the audience. Here, one merely imitates the outward behaviour (gestures, etc.) and not the concurrent emotional states. This visible gap between the outward gestures, etc. and the supposed emotional states occasions amusement.

We may go back to the question as to the emotion we experience in the context of a dramatic characters or situation. Take, for example, the character Anna Karenina in the novel and the pity we feel for her. Is this emotion real? The question assumes importance because Anna Karenina is a make-believe character in a make-believe work of art. But in this example, our feeling of pity for the character Anna Karenina is real that you make-believe because we pretend to ourselves that what we are reading about or watching in the film is a real Anna Karenina. Our original belief that the work was fiction would be overlaid with the active pretence that it is real while we attend to it. Such reality would indeed be of a different order, because it has a "closed" form that is invested with a degree of finality. So our response would be in the context of this universe of discourse that has its own autonomy. A work of art has its own autonomy as it exists and sustains itself in terms of its own internal structure and the elements therein. So the pity we feel for Anna Karenina is with reference to Anna in the novel. This is quite unlike the pity we might feel for the roadside beggar as here we have no knowledge about the beggar's life as a whole.

In one sense perhaps, art appears more real than life. Each detail or element in it is completely relevant and significant to the whole work. In responding to a work of art, we respond to the whole structure in terms of all its elements in their relationship to each other, inter se. But in real life, our responses are mostly to individual elements/incidents without necessarily having to reconstruct a whole context to it. And, what is more, even when we imaginatively reconstruct a whole context, it necessarily lacks finality or a closed form. In contrast, works of art present for our envisagement is a closed and final form with an "end" to it. Whatever be our psychological responses in the context of art, it does not call for any action or reaction.

In sharp focus, we are making the following points: (a) while responding to a work of art, we respond to the idea of a whole complex structure of the work in terms of all its internal parts. (b) And, in responding to the "whole", which appears invested with finality, our psychological reactions rid themselves of any desire or motivation for intervening in the matter. As the consequences of (a) and (b), the psychological reactions such as fear, pity, etc. are felt with a more vivid and full-blown character without their burden felt on our motor responses. In this context, a very useful distinction has been drawn between the imaginary and the fictional (by Dammann 1992).[5] This distinction helps us to understand our responses to fiction. One can imagine an event without being moved at all, but a fictional event/character evokes emotions sometimes intense and powerful. The key point here is that fiction provides a context and perspective for one to respond to it in terms of some emotion.

It is necessary to understand the distinction between imagination and fiction. Indeed, fiction is a product of imagination. But it is much more than that. Fiction represents an autonomous whole in which the parts are related to each other. So when we are moved to tears at some characters' fate in the novel or film, our response is to that character in the fiction that is related to the characters and situations in the fiction. Fiction provides an autonomous context of its own, and all the details such as characters, events, etc. are integrally related to the total structure of the work. This also accounts for the fact that only a good or successful work of art with its unified structure is capable of evoking psychological reactions such as are under consideration. If the work does not hang together as a unified whole, it remains a weak work and is hardly capable of evoking any response on the part of the audience. Mere imagination, on the other hand, cannot be treated as a work of art as it lacks any well-integrated structure.

In the foregoing discussion, we have pressed into service the concept of "pretence" and have gone on to draw a distinction between "pretending to oneself" and

---

[5] For although I may be moved by imagining that my house is on fire, or that someone had committed suicide, or been strangled by an unjustifiably jealous husband, I would probably be moved, or at any rate more moved, by putting that event into some kind of context. For it is quite possible to imagine such events without being moved at all. The thought of my house being on fire is more likely to move me because the context in which I place this imagined event (destruction of what has given my life meaning or whatever). I am, in other words, imagining story, a fiction. The imaginary moves more the closer it moves towards the fictional.

'pretending to others". In common usage, it is the latter that is generally in use, for pretending is commonly taken to be in relation to others. In such cases, there is an overtone of a disparaging or pejorative sense as it calls for an active participation in an act of deceit. It is always accompanied by an ulterior motive to deceive the other person. We generally do not take very kindly to such attempts at pretending to others. In short, "pretending to others" involves putting up an appearance which is at variance with what is really the case. That is to say, that there is a deliberate attempt to create a gulf between reality and appearance. And this is done for the sake of the pretender's own personal benefit, gain or advantage.

Now, in the case of creative endeavour, appearance is its reality; there is no identity other than what the appearance is. For the actor that plays out a role in a film or drama, he creates an appearance that is not his true self. Yet, that role alone is real and not his actual character. In his pretence to himself, he forgets or "suspends" for the occasion his true self; he acts on the role of that character as if he was really that character. The concept of "pretending to oneself", to our mind, is useful as it precludes the possibility of art being equated to deception. Thus, "pretending to oneself" consists really being what one is pretending to be. When, say, the actor is pretending to herself that she is Anna Karenina, she is being as though the real Anna Karenina, feeling inwardly also that she is the real Anna Karenina. This, indeed, is the hallmark of a great or successful actor. For such an artist, the logical divide between fact and fiction no longer operates.

Now in view of this the question of truth in literature assumes relevance as literature is *about* life. It has been even held by some thinkers that literature "mirrors" life. Let us try and understand this in perspective. If we turn back to Plato's charge against literature, it is crucial to understand that for Plato the life as we experience through our senses is not "real". On this view, literature will have no contact with "reality". So, one would argue that art or literature can only mislead us about what is true or real. Plato looks down upon poetry with contempt on the ground that it takes us away from the metaphysical world of reality. In this sense, literature and philosophy stand in opposition to each other. The opposition becomes sharper when literature is regarded as a vehicle of emotions.[6] Now we may elaborate the point further. For Plato, the domain of truth or reality represents suprasensuous order of existence. The world that is given to us by the senses is only an imperfect copy of reality. Literature imitates the world of senses and takes us farther away from the real. While philosophy is a search for truth or reality, literature is identified with *falsehood*. Further, it has been argued that literature or art generally evokes emotions in the mind of the reader. So, one cannot carry out the search for truth. Besides its fictional elements, literature for its emotive nature stands opposed to philosophy. Plato sets literature and philosophy so far apart that difference between literature as falsehood and philosophy as truth remains irresolvable.

However, it must be noted that in the context of the Western tradition, it was Aristotle who answers many of the objections that Plato raises against art and litera-

---

[6] As Morris Weitz sums up this point: "Literature can no more be married to philosophy than falsehood can to truth." (Weitz 1983, p. 4).

ture by pointing out that its emotive content is quite able to represent truth of our life of emotion. His theory of "catharsis" relating to the purging of harmful and negative emotions such as pity and fear was a great leap towards recognizing literature as a vehicle of truth. Interestingly, earlier in the twentieth century, I.A. Richards and the logical positivists have indicted literature on the ground that truth and literature are far apart as the latter carries emotive elements. The argument is roughly as follows. Linguistic sentences in science are statements that are affirmed either as true or false. But sentences in literature are not affirmed as true or false. So these sentences cannot be regarded as statements.[7]

For the logical positivists, on the other hand, a dilemma presents itself. According to them, meaningfulness of a sentence depends on its truth-value conditions. Now for sentences in literature, truth-value conditions cannot be laid down, and so, these are to be regarded as no better than emotive ejaculations, more like Oh! Ah! and so on. It is interesting to note here that for Wittgenstein, philosophy plays a therapeutic role rather than a theory or doctrinal truth. From this perspective, the idea of philosophy in literature is nonsense. The matter is put by Morris Weitz as follows: "That there is no such thing as philosophy in literature is no true or false doctrine either; rather it serves as a reminder of the inability of philosophy to function in a doctrinal capacity and as a further reminder of the function of sentences in literature. It is therefore, on Wittgenstein's view, philosophy is nonsense, not literature" (Weitz 1983, p. 34).

We may now put the arguments briefly. Literature cannot claim to contain truth as it deals with unreal characters and situations. This is based on the argument that statements in works of literature do not have any truth-value. Further, sentences in literature are pseudo-statements; these are no different from emotive ejaculations to which no truth or falsity can be ascribed. Finally, philosophy being an activity (doing philosophy) and not a theory, philosophy in literature is nonsense. Those who advance such arguments foreclose on the possibility of joining literature and philosophy.[8] As against such a view, we would argue that it is important to take into account what literature actively does to or for us and how it does this.

Now in this context the question arises: How do we understand this concept of "make-belief" or "pretence", in relation to other arts such as novel, painting, musical performance and so on? How would the concept of "pretending to oneself" apply in such instances? There is indeed another way of understanding the concept which would prove more helpful. Let us put it as follows. A work of art is a unified structure in which the parts or elements are related to one another as well as related to the whole in an organic relationship. This invests every part within it with a degree of relevance and significance. In other words, the total structure of the work

---

[7] I.A. Richards has the following to say: "It will be admitted – by those who distinguish between scientific statement where truth is ultimately a matter of verification as this is understood in the laboratory, and a emotive utterance, where 'truth' is primarily acceptability *by* some attitude, and more remotely is the acceptability of this attitude itself – that it is *not* the poet's business to make the scientific statements. Yet poetry has constantly the air of making statements, and important ones; which is one reason why some mathematicians cannot read it." (Richards 1970, p. 568).

[8] Also, for an interesting discussion on the uses of fiction in analytically oriented philosophers' writings, see Anderson (1992, pp. 203–213).

of art provides the relevant context in relation to which the parts or details in it must appear relevant and meaningful. Thus when the internal structure of a work of art reveals a high degree of coherence, the gap between "is" and "seems" will disappear; what it seems is what it really is. Precisely this objective is achieved when we say that in a dramatic performance or film, the actor has to pretend to himself to be the character he is playing. So in the case of a work of art, what it seems is what it is; there is no gap between appearance and reality.

Our use of the expressions "pretending to others" and "pretending to oneself" is only to draw an important distinction as to how the "make-believe" is so radically and significantly different from ordinary cases of pretence, deception, illusion, etc. that one uses in everyday life. The use of the expression "pretending to oneself", though somewhat confusing and not a happy one either, is made in order to focus on the distinction between life and art. The thrust of the argument is that the make-believe that is created in art is not for the sake of others. Nor is there an intention on the part of the artist to deceive the audience. The objective here is to create a conception of life or organic whole as such by the use of the device of selectivity and relevancy.

The important point we are making here is that the conception of life that is created in a novel or film is such that it seems complete and final. The distinction between "seems" and "is" no longer can sustain itself, and it breaks down. What seems is all that there is. Now how does this distinction break down? In the first place, the reader or audience is aware that what happens in the novel or the film is not in continuity with what happens in life regardless of the degree of similarity between the two. The important distinction between the creative realm and everyday life is that the events, situations and characters in a novel or film seem manifestly and interminably connected though in life this is not the case. We encounter events and situations without necessarily having a sense of any connectivity between them. The creative realm, on the other hand, presents a complete world with its own autonomy where everything has a clear and visible relevance to the created whole. This is, indeed, what may be called "second-order" world with its own finality and form; there is nothing that seems unconnected here. Every detail in it seems relevant and connected to the total work. For example, in a novel, every event is transparently connected with every other event or character in some way. It assumes a "closed" form and has a degree of "finality". This may also be described, for the same reason, a "make-believe" world or fiction. In contrast, we do not confront situations and events with any sense of apparent necessity or finality. Only much later, when we reflect on what we have experienced in life, we might find some connectedness in them.

This matter has been explained by Susanne K. Langer (1953, p. 40) in the following manner. According to her, art creates "symbolic" representation of the "forms of feeling"; and, literature, in particular, creates "semblance" of felt or experienced life. Briefly, this may be understood as follows. The work of art is a "symbol" the function of which is to evoke in the mind of the reader or onlooker a conception of life. According to her, this becomes possible as art represents symbolically the logical structure of the life of feeling. Further, in the case of literature rather than imitating the external appearances, the creative writer weaves together an analogue of the internal life feeling. Even though the characters, situations, etc. are unreal or imaginary, these are so well integrated into the total work so as to create a semblance of felt life. It is important to note here that by the term "feeling", Langer does not mean any particular emotion. For her, "feeling" stands for the way life in general is experienced. Implicit here is the notion of "form" or "structure" that describe the way we feel life as such. By way of illustration, one can imagine a dry river bed which bears on the sand bed the marks and imprint of the way that water has flown down it. Quite in the same fashion, our lived life also leaves behind a "form" by way of its imprint. Creative arts have their engagement with such "forms of life". It is indeed the internal structure of life that is apprehended, and its analogue is created in literature. Finally, and most importantly, the emergent created work shines forth as a "symbol" in the sense that it does *not* refer to anything *other than itself*. This self-referent symbol is such that the reader may grasp intuitively knowledge about emotions in life. The fictional elements in it do not take us away from the truth or reality about life as it is presented in the work. Interestingly, these elements intensify reality and make it "more perceivable".[9]

While it is true that life provides the raw material, as it were, for the creation of art (novel, film, etc.), what holds the various elements together by a relation of necessity is its fictionality or make-believe character. There is nothing outside of this make-believe world, and so our response to it assumes contemplative measure. It demands attention that must be exclusive to it whereby the viewer suspends consideration of anything outside of it. Further, because of the apparent inseparability of its various elements within (situations, characters, events, etc.) the fictional work, it demands attention which must be free from the burden of carrying on any action in response to whatever is presented in it. While attending to the work, we do not allow the awareness of the outside world around to obtrude upon our response to it. This created work assumes autonomy for itself as it does not allow the outside world into it. The unbridgeable distinction between life and fiction stands out very clearly. We confront life in terms of events that are contingent in nature, and while experiencing them, we do not necessarily see or feel any connection between them. Each event hangs out individually, and we respond to them. Our responses to them call upon us to react in various ways to their consequences or effect in our personal life. Thus we may try and want to alter, modify, change or prolong the event depending on the way it affects us.

In the case of a fictional work, each event or situation in it is unalterable or is given with a stamp of finality about it. There seems to be a relation of necessity that binds all the events (or parts thereof) together leaving no scope for anyone to intervene or change the course of events. The finality of the form of a fictional work or the degree of necessity underlying it puts the reader or spectator in a contemplative mode of response; thus discontinuity or distinctiveness between the two realms, that is, life and fiction, must be sustained in a conscious and deliberate manner. Any intermixing of the two would hamper our aesthetic response. For example, while witnessing a street-corner play on some social issue, we get so much carried away

[9] Also, for a fuller discussion on some of these aspects, see Ghosh (1979).

by it that we get into a reactive mode of behaviour and try to intervene in the proceedings. It will be a case of conflating the two domains of life and make-believe world, and our response to the play will not qualify as of aesthetic or contemplative mode.

Our responses to a work of art are given only in a reflective mode of consciousness that precludes the possibility and scope for behaving in normal reactive frame of mind. So, even if we experience anger or sadness as a response to a creative work, we do so in relation to the make-believe world which thereby precludes us from reacting to them as though it was happening in real life. While seeing the villain plot against the protagonist in a film, we might actually feel anger and/or fear but do not make any intervention against the same. The feeling is experienced as real, but it remains delinked from our usual behavioural orientation.

We have argued that the fictional world created in a novel or film assumes a sense of finality such that everything is related to everything in it by what might seem a relation of necessity. It is a closed form in which nothing is contingent as everything within it is bound together by a necessary relation. Given the pervading sense of finality about a work of art, and in the specific instance of fiction or film, the viewer must accept the work for what it is in which no alteration is called for. Thus a situation presented in this kind of work has to be viewed in relation to its own context, i.e. in the context of the whole film or novel. We would argue, therefore, that our feeling of, say, fear or anger in the context of the novel or film is both *real* and *rational* in so far as it is occasional by the work of art.

Philosophical discussions about the notions of truth and fiction in the context of literature have assumed importance in recent years. It has been generally argued that fiction adds to the value of the literary work. Fiction in literature makes it possible for an imaginative reader to get an insight into life as such. Julian Mitchell makes the following pertinent point: "Fiction is a way – or it can be a way – of knowing the whole lives of people, of compressing information by compressing time" (Mitchell 1973, p. 17). Further, "imagination is a way of perceiving... And if we can talk about the truth and falsehood of other impressions, then we can talk of the truth and falsehood of imaginative ones too" (Mitchell 1973, p. 22). And, finally, "we judge books by life and other books: we judge life by books and other life. Fiction can be as true as anything else" (Mitchell 1973). Fiction functions in a significant way that brings into sharp focus whole lives in a condensed manner. In short, fiction particularizes reality with the help of details that are unreal and imaginary. Thus, Dilman argues that literature brings out truth about life as "the literary writer's concerns... is with *the particular*, he is concerned to see things in their particularity, to capture and convey this in his work" (Dilman 1993, p. 27). So what literature does is to *show* life and emotion in the work rather than state it.

It would be worthwhile to point out that many a time either the created work is such that it does not hang together and thus turn out to be a weak or unsuccessful work or alternatively, the audience conflates the make-believe character of the work with real-life situation. This results in the audience taking on a reactive mode as is the case of confronting with life situations. Many of the controversies that arise in the context of novels/films, etc. are due to either of these two reasons. When in a reactive mode of encounter with objects, situations and characters in life, these remain transcendent to our consciousness, that is to say, outside of us. But in the context of creative works, there is a process of inwardization on the part of the audience which makes the emotions more perceivable and intense. So we do not react to situations presented in a novel or film, rather we begin to develop a deep understanding about life and its internal structures. Here, emotions themselves are the object of our contemplation.[10] To feel an emotion in its purity is having not to get involved with its effect or consequence in our individual life. Rather, it is to understand the emotion internally by reflecting on it. We would conclude the discussion by making the following points. In the first place, the emotions experienced in relation to events characters, etc. in a fictional work (say, novel, film, etc.) are real and not "make-believe", even though these psychological responses are not accompanied by the belief as to the reality of the characters or events to which such responses are directed. Secondly, the fictional work is invested with a degree of finality and closure such that it makes possible suspension of any reactive mode on the part of the reader/viewer. Thus these feelings (such as anger, fear, etc.) are experienced without their attendant consequences and the anticipated reactions thereto. The emotions so experienced are rational as their occurrence is occasioned by the specific context of the created work. Fictionality of the work is the enabling factor in compressing a whole life into a span of a few hundred pages or a few hours whereby it enables the reader or spectator to reflect on such life and emotions. Finally, feelings evoked by the make-believe realm are "free" in as much as these are not linked to the consequences that normally follow in everyday life. These feelings can be savoured without being affected by their attendant consequence and the anticipated reaction threats.

References

Anderson, S. L. (1992, July). Philosophy and fiction. *Metaphilosophy, 23*(3).

Dammann, R. M. J. (1992, January). Emotion and fiction. *The British Journal of Aesthetics, 32.*

Dilman, I. (July 1993). Art and reality: Some reflections on the arts. *Philosophical Investigations, 18*, 3.

Ghosh, R. K. (1979). *Aesthetic theory and art: A study in Susanne K. Langer.* Delhi: Ajanta Publications.

Krishna, D. (1989). Art and the cognitive enterprise with the actual world. In *The art of the conceptual: Exploration in a conceptual maze over three decades.* Delhi: ICPR.

Langer, S. K. (1953). *Feeling and form.* New York: Routledge/Kegan Paul.

McCormick, P. (1988). *Fiction, philosophies, and the problems of poetics.* Cornell University Press.

---

[10] As Daya Krishna remarks: "In art, the function of the imagination has been primarily conceived as not giving us truth or helping in the exploration of truth, but basically as creating a world which is essentially different from the world as it is actually there. It is so to say, the creation of a second order world which has a reality of its own but which has no relation except that of indirect derivation with the actual world" (Krishna 1989, p. 126, emphases added).

Mitchell, Julian, "Truth and fiction", *Philosophy and the arts: Royal institute of philosophical lectures*, 1971–72 Vol 10 Macmillan, 1973.

Neil, A. (Winter, 1991). Fear, fiction and make-belief. *The Journal of Aesthetics and Art Criticism, 49*(1).

New, C. (1999). *Philosophy of literature: An introduction*. Routledge.

Richards, I. A. (1970). Poetry and beliefs. In M. Weitz (Ed.), *Problems in aesthetics* (2nd ed.). Macmillan.

Walton, K. (1978). Fearing fiction. *Journal of Philosophy, 75*.

Weitz, M. (1983). Literature and philosophy. In J. P. Strelka (Ed.), *Literary criticism and philosophy*. Pennsylvania.

Chapter 4
Literature and Life

Abstract The chapter deals with the relation between literature and life. A literary work is to be viewed in its totality and for the quality of experience it evokes. Literature borrows elements from life, but it creates an autonomous domain that is invested with an uncommon import. For that matter, a literary work being in the nature of fiction performs the useful task of making sense of life as such and makes us see it in a new perspective. It is argued that even though the domain of artistic creation is autonomous in character, it helps one to make sense of life. There is also discussed here the alleged opposition between literature and philosophy and that while literature deals with a fictional world, the main concern of philosophy is truth. It has been pointed out that literature makes available to us the truth about life by presenting it as a "closed form" exemplifying the internal coherence and connectedness of various elements in it.

Keywords Literary form · Symbol · Presentational symbol · Closed form ·
Meaning and import

What does a literary text stand for? What is its relation to life and world? These questions have undoubtedly a bearing on literary aesthetics. Let us begin by asking: what is the function of a literary text as a work of art? Broadly speaking, we may make the following points in response to this question. In the first place, it is capable of arresting our attention in a way that most other things do not, and such attention is not for the sake of any ulterior purpose. Secondly, it makes us reflect on the meaning or significance of the work. And, finally, it is also capable of providing a special kind of satisfaction when its meaning or import is duly grasped. This has to do with imparting a perspective with which to look at life as such. Of the three points indicated above, the second one presents a problematic. Quite understandably, a work may be considered from various viewpoints, and so, it may have several different interpretations. For example, a student of history or sociology may read into the work some meaning or value from their perspective, but this will be quite independent of the aesthetic merit of the work. We would thus qualify the aesthetic value of a literary work quite independently of its other dimensions. The sociological or historical inputs that may be gleaned from, say, a novel, does not count for its aesthetic value. It is in this sense that the work's *autonomy* is to be reached into. For example, when we read Bankim Chandra Chattopadhyay's *Anandamath*, we are struck by the nationalist mood and aspiration of the times. But the aesthetic merit of this great work transcends any such inputs. What is it that is aesthetically to be regarded as its value?

Now there is indeed a long tradition in the philosophy of art that supports the view that each artwork is autonomous as it enjoys its own internal integrity. In the words of Carl R. Hausman, "The meanings and what the work may refer to are integral to the work itself. By contrast, a practical sign need not have a form that is unique in the way it informs us of what it refers to. A barber pole is only one way to refer to a barber shop, and its form is used only as a device or vehicle to tell us what is behind the door where it appears. ... But a Monet painting of water lilies has a form that is *indispensible* in offering us the significance of the work" (Hausman 1986, pp. 163–4).

Hausman holds the view that the self-referential character is what distinguishes a work of art. It primarily and essentially refers to itself. He goes on to suggest that when the work shows some extra-aesthetic human experience or quality, it is possible to do so only in and through the aesthetic domain. So a work of art may sometimes give us an insight about the world in and through its aesthetic aspect. But this in no way goes against the autonomy thesis. Thus when, say, a novel or a short story is shown to be set in a particular sociocultural milieu, that becomes only incidental to it as a literary text and its aesthetic value. On the same grounds, a newspaper report about some incident is not to be regarded as a literary text though it can be something on which a story or novel may be based. The literary text must hold itself out on its aesthetic merit and not by virtue of the incident or situation it is based on. The self-referential nature of an aesthetic object is also brought out forcefully by Susanne K. Langer[1] who distinguishes between discursive symbol and "presentational symbol" while arguing that a work of art is a case of "presentational symbol". The latter only stands for "no other than itself". It is interesting to note how a distinction is drawn between language on the one hand and art on the other hand. Language is a system of symbols in which each word stands for or refers to something other than itself. A word refers to an object, event or situation. Art, on the other hand, refers only to itself. It may be regarded as a symbol of human emotion. Literary text is a case of "presentational symbol" even though the words used in it may constitute a system of discursive symbols. A fuller discussion on this may await until later.

However, there have been attempts to debunk the "autonomy" thesis, and in recent times a philosophical critique of this thesis has been presented by Nick McAdoo.[2] He has raised some seminal issues concerning the self-referential nature of a work of art. He argues that the aesthetic and the extra-aesthetic coalesce together such that it is not quite possible to pull them apart. He goes on to argue that a proper

---

[1] Langer (1953) (Her central thesis has been developed here).

[2] McAdoo (1992). For a detailed critical analysis of the point raised by McAdoo, see also Ghosh (1996).

understanding of the aesthetic import would be possible only if one has knowledge about the world and everyday life. For him, the aesthetic domain and the world around collapse into one such that it is not really possible to distinguish the worlds apart. Such a view indeed has serious implications for our aesthetic discourse.

So it would be worthwhile to turn to a brief examination of this view against the autonomy thesis. McAdoo proceeds by stating that there is no "rigid [,] either/or distinction between aesthetic purity and worldly significance" (McAdoo 1992, p. 135) since attributions to works of art are made by the use of both "aesthetic" and "nonaesthetic" words in the language. Let us put the matter in this way. We talk about a work of art by using words like "sad", "profound", "placid", "dynamic", etc. that are used in the context of everyday life as also words like "graceful", "delicate", "discordant", "elegant" and so on that are generally used to refer to the aesthetic dimension. Thus words as "sad" and "profound" are used as much in the context of everyday life experiences as for, say, musical compositions or poems and novels. Similarly, one may point out that the supposedly aesthetic term like "graceful" usually used in the context of dance movements is also pressed into service to talk about one's "graceful" manners, etc. in the context of everyday life situation. McAdoo's argument is based on such usages and puts forward the point that the separation of two exclusive domains, aesthetic and nonaesthetic, is not warranted on this ground.

The crux of his argument here is that the divide and the attendant tension in this regard must go as, according to McAdoo, the so-called aesthetic words derive their usage from the use of these terms in the everyday life context. To put it differently, all these words are used primarily for everyday life situations and thus find their way into the vocabulary of terms for their use in the context of aesthetic domain. In other words, there is no exclusive domain such as the aesthetic that may be regarded as quite distinguishably apart from life or world. McAdoo considers the use of words such as "graceful", "elegant", etc. which find their use only in aesthetic discourse. He raises the question, "whether such words can be fully understood without evoking extra-aesthetic associations, especially in so far as, to state the obvious, such qualities do not exist per se, but only in their perceptual instantiations, which are to be found just as much in the real world as in works of art" (McAdoo 1992, p. 136) For McAdoo, whatever attributions are made for a work of art, it derives it from the vocabulary used for the everyday life and world. The philosophical implication of this position is that the aesthetic discourse can become intelligible only by means of words that are used in the everyday life. This indeed leads to a piquant situation in which the divide between art and life seems to fall through. If it is held that whatever is allegedly aesthetic is not discontinuous with life on the ground, as it is argued by McAdoo, and that our everyday language is adequate for describing artworks, then there would be no legitimacy for describing something as a work of art. But it does not need reiteration that we *do* hold a class of objects or events as falling under the rubric term "art". McAdoo's argument goes against such a commonly accepted standpoint.

We may now turn to a critical assessment of the situation. In the first place, we must view art as *discontinuous* with life, or else we could not claim to respond to a certain class of things such as novels, poems, sculptures, paintings, etc. aesthetically.

Undeniably, such artistic creations are often a source of aesthetic delight when considered in a contemplative mode. In other words, such objects qua art are not used or put to any utilitarian end. This is not to say that some utilitarian objects can never be viewed aesthetically. Finest examples of such cases are instances of *Dada* art. Celebrated artist Marcel Duchamp tellingly made the point by using a castaway urinal and putting it forth as an official entry in the art exhibition (*Fountain*). But the underlying point here is that utilitarian perspective and aesthetic mode of contemplation are mutually exclusive of each other. What is viewed aesthetically cannot at the same time be regarded from the utilitarian angle. The point that needs to be stressed here is this. Viewing things in aesthetic mode provides us with a special kind of satisfaction that is quite distinctive in itself. Such aesthetic satisfaction is quite independent of and different from the utilitarian value of the object. For example, the publisher who brings out a novel or some literary work has his primary interest in, say, the commercial gains from its sale though the primary interest of the reader lies in the aesthetic merit and the resultant experience that he derives from the literary work. It is quite another matter that without its aesthetic merit, the published novel will not sell and its commercial value will be at a low. So an aesthetic object (novel, painting, etc.) may have some commercial gain accruing from it, but the two domains are distinctly different from each other. Thus McAdoo's argument that art and life do not represent two distinctive domains does not seem warranted. Our point here is that when a thing is viewed aesthetically it ceases for that moment to participate as an object of utility. One can *either* regard an object as of aesthetic contemplation *or* as one of utility. The ontological status of the aesthetic object precludes it from being anything other than an object of pure contemplation. In a novel, for example, the events, situations and characters may quite possibly bear some resemblance to real life. But what we appreciate aesthetically is not these elements *as such* but the way they have been configured into an aesthetically appealing *form*. Looking at from this perspective, it has nothing to do with whether or not such resemblance is faithful to the element in real life. Thus it makes sense to distinguish between aspects that may be characterized as purely aesthetic and those that are not (i.e. nonaesthetic).

It may be noted here in the passing that even with regard to the concept of aesthetic experience, there has been a tendency among many of the analytic philosophers to debunk it by arguing that there is no specific experience of this kind. The hardcore analytic philosopher holds the view that such experience cannot be talked about in objective terms.[3] On the contrary, such an approach persuades one to talk you out of it even if you show any inclination to reflect on the kind of experience one may have from watching a movie, reading a novel or listening to music.

Now, McAdoo's emphatic assertion that "the work's aesthetic form must presuppose extra-aesthetic knowledge" (McAdoo 1992, p. 131) seems misplaced. For it is not true that our appreciation of "aesthetic form" is not qualitatively guided or determined by our ability to perceive life elements in the work of art. Please recall here the point made by Clive Bell according to whom "to appreciate a work of art we

---

[3] For a discussion on this, please see Mitias (1986).

need bring with us nothing from life… nothing but a sense of form and colour and knowledge of three-dimensional space"[4] Even though McAdoo has himself quoted these lines, he fails to see the underlying point. It is important to see that appreciating a work of art does not have anything to do with finding resemblances to life and world. One may imagine works of art that bear no resemblances to life. But these would be appreciated for their aesthetic merit. Examples of such cases of art would include abstract paintings, pure musical compositions and even abstract literature.

The purist has no quarrel with the representational elements in a work of art. Nor does non-representational works run a handicapped race with regard to their appreciation for aesthetic value. For example, one may enjoy a piece of abstract painting as well as a representational landscape painting. Aesthetic appreciation of a work of art is not to be confused with mere recognition of life elements in it. Why would we otherwise distinguish between a piece of creative writing and mere newspaper report which is based on some actual incident? We might ask in the same vain as to the grounds on which to distinguish between good art and bad or mediocre art.

Now McAdoo seems to anticipate such difficulties and so he works out a somewhat different strategy to counter the argument raised here. So he goes on to argue that "even while seeing the work as pure 'presence' we have also to judge its extra-aesthetic content quite differently i.e. as a more or less successful attempt to portray an instance of something in the world and therefore subject to determinate truth-conditions" (McAdoo 1992, p. 132). But this hardly is of any help to us. What does he really mean by "extra-aesthetic content" as also for that matter by "truth-conditions"? How, for example, you would appreciate Picasso's *Guernica* on the basis of "truth-condition"? One may or may not be familiar with the political turmoil in Spain at that time to be able to respond aesthetically to the painting inspired by the civil war around that time. Indeed, there is no "extra-aesthetic" content that must bear to bring upon our appreciation of this celebrated painting. These conditions would render themselves quite irrelevant and inconsequential in aesthetically enjoying a novel or a story even if it be claimed to have been inspired by some real-life situation. Obviously, we do not judge the work on such grounds.

There is another approach that McAdoo takes in support of his view. This has to do with the way we may talk about the business of describing the aspects of a work of art by demolishing the dichotomy between aesthetic and nonaesthetic terms that are used in such descriptions. He argues that the aesthetic terms also have their home in nonaesthetic terms and that the former would make sense only from their relation to the nonaesthetic terms. Further, that the idea of "pure" aesthetic form or property is not tenable as these terms do not exist in isolated and mutually exclusive domains. Take, for example, the statement "the music is sad". McAdoo argues that the appraisal term "sad" is used because nonaesthetic term ("sad") is tied up inseparably with the aesthetic situation. We do not posit a new meaning for "sad". He argues that words like "sad", "profound", etc. have their primary home in the everyday nonaesthetic world. He points out that nonaesthetic words like "sad" can be used for the aesthetic work only because the nonaesthetic qualities are to be found

---

[4] As quoted by McAdoo (1992, p. 131).

given inseparably with the aesthetic qualities. He draws support from Roger Scruton by referring to his view. "The use [of 'sad'] to refer to an emotional state is primary, and anyone who did not understand this use of the term 'sad' – did not understand what the emotion of sadness was – would not know what he was talking about in attributing sadness to a work of art" (Scruton 1974, p. 38).

Interestingly, McAdoo grants that the use of such terms ("sad", "profound", etc.) is made in the "extended" sense as "the sad aspect is linked to a feeling of contemplative aesthetic pleasure rather than a stimulus to action" (McAdoo 1992, p. 134). But he stops short of developing the point to its logical conclusion. Responding to his point, we may ask the following. Why does he not see that only such aspects as are given in the aesthetic mode stand distinguishably apart from the nonaesthetic aspects? Therefore, McAdoo's refusal to grant an independent and autonomous status to the "pure" aesthetic domain is quite unwarranted. The purported "extended" sense of the term "sad" in the context of an artwork he refers to must necessarily presuppose a "pure" and aesthetic domain that we may talk about. The term is borrowed from the everyday world vocabulary, and its use is extended to the aesthetic domain in a metaphorical sense. Sadness in music is for sure not the same as it stands for in the everyday context. As an aesthetic quality, sadness is a source of delight which definitely is not the case in the everyday life.

And, now for the purely aesthetic terms like "graceful", "beautiful", etc., McAdoo argues that the use and application of such words in our language is a matter of learning the same in our childhood as we begin to respond to the world around. These words are used to describe the everyday experiences of life. The child learns to point to a flower and describe it as beautiful or a cat as graceful. McAdoo's argument here seems to be that based on such linguistic practices in the process of learning a language, we are also capable of describing aesthetic qualities in terms of the everyday language. This, for him, is the justification for not upholding a "pure" aesthetic domain. Now by way of rejoinder, we might as well turn the argument on its head. The words "beautiful" and "graceful" are used to describe, say, flowers and cats precisely for these aesthetic elements to be present in our surroundings. The gracefulness in a cat is an aesthetic quality, and similarly, the beautiful is an aesthetic aspect of a flower. This would only reinforce our point that aesthetic qualities are to be found all around us in terms of everything that we confront in the everyday life which in turn does inspire some of us to "create" an aesthetic domain in and through some physical medium. No way does it take away from the exclusivity and autonomy of art world.

McAdoo's position when put in simple terms is as follows. Our understanding and use of the words by which we describe the aesthetic aspects and qualities depend on our knowledge about and familiarity with nonaesthetic situations. So he would have us conclude from this that both "aesthetic form and worldly significance would seem to be ultimately inseparable". He disagrees with the view of Peter Kivy according to whom "the expressive properties of music alone are purely musical properties, understandable in purely musical terms" (Kivy 1990, p. 195). For McAdoo there are no such properties. He seeks to build up the case that even the use of aesthetic terms is learnt through their use in the context of the everyday world. But McAdoo seems to have no satisfactory explanation for the "collapse" of the two worlds—the aesthetic and the nonaesthetic. The point that we would stress here is this. We commend a work of art, of whatever kind, not for what it refers to outside of the work, but rather for what it is in *itself*. This is also the point made by the formalist as Clive Bell speaks of "knowledge of three-dimensional space" or "a sense of form and colour" that alone would be relevant to our appreciation of a work of art. This is not to suggest that such knowledge is possible without direct experience of life and world. But the underlying idea is that for appreciation of a work of art, no *special* kind of knowledge about the world is presupposed. On the other hand, our response to a work of art would be enhanced if we have an intimate knowledge of the medium in which the work is executed. When a novelist writes a novel, it is inevitable that he would draw a great deal from his/her own vast experience of life and world. But he presents in the novel not his mere collection of these facts of experience. So the reader is under no obligation to have first-hand knowledge of these facts. What he responds to is a creative *form* whereby he is able to have an insight into some aspect of life and world. Such insights also provide a sense of delectation which we cherish in the literary work. Even if it be the case that the work relates to some special aspect of life experience, what comes for aesthetic appreciation is the way the experience is depicted.

So the purist who talks about a pure aesthetic domain has no quarrel with the elements of life being presented in the work of art. Take, for example, the Ray film *Pather Panchali* which is set in the background of rural Bengal which received universal acclaim because of its cinematic qualities even though the Western audiences did not have any direct knowledge or experience of the life elements present in the movie or story. Thus it is nobody's case that in order to have aesthetic delight, one must be totally cut off from the world. A fair assessment of the formalist's position must guard against any such distorted view. The point that we are stressing here is that there is indeed an aesthetic domain which pulls us to respond to a work of art. The aesthetic domain, on our view, represents *value* rather than facts. Quite understandably, therefore, the philosopher of the analytic persuasion finds it problematic to negotiate with the aesthetic value within the given everyday linguistic practices. McAdoo's attempt to conflate the two domains of value and fact in terms of the linguistic matrix is symptomatic of an approach to reduce *value* to fact. In the process it knocks at the basis of the claim for aesthetic experience that is characterized by a sense of delight.

It is in this context that it is pertinent to ask the question, what is the relation between art and life? We would try and understand this in the context of literary arts, in particular, though the same considerations would apply to any form of art such as plastic arts, cinematic/dramatic arts, musical performances and so on. We might begin with a preliminary remark by way of saying that understanding art is not purely a cognitive exercise. Further, we must begin by clarifying the distinction between art (both literary and non-literary) on the one hand and language on the other hand. Language is used as a cognitive tool to understand the world. The structure of our everyday language helps us to abbreviate world for our understanding. In this process, language represents reality for us and is thus said to function as a "symbol". According to Susanne K. Langer, language may be regarded as "discursive symbol" while she goes on to distinguish it from art which is termed as "presentational" (nondiscursive) symbol. What it boils down to saying is that art, too, functions as a symbol which is defined by her as "the creation of forms symbolic of human feeling" (Langer 1953, p. 40). It is quite useful to understand the distinction between the two kinds of symbol. This also would help us clarify the "autonomy" thesis about art. The main point of distinction between "discursive" and "nondiscursive" symbol is that language as a system of discursive symbols refers to something other than itself, whereas art as a symbol refers to *nothing other than itself*.

It is now important to understand the nature of the autonomous domain in the case of the literary arts. Langer goes on to say that each art form is characterized by a distinctive element. For example, in painting what is created may be said to be "virtual space", in sculpture it is "virtual volume", in music it is "virtual time", and so, in literature it is "virtual life". In other words, even if it be said that art in some sense may represent life, one must distinguish between the everyday life or real life and "virtual life". Undoubtedly, there is some relation between life as it is experienced in the everyday context and life that is "created" in and through literature. For that matter, it is relevant to ask why it is regarded as "virtual" in character. According to Langer, the distinction between the two kinds of life has to do with the *way* life is represented in literature. Indeed, the latter has a definitive *form* of its own ("virtual life") which has at least two distinctive characteristics, namely, finality and transparency. Life is open-ended, but the life represented in the literary work is a "closed" one, as it has a degree of finality about it. The sequence of events and characters in a novel are unalterable and are put together in a certain configuration that bears the stamp of finality. Also, within the parameter of the closed form, nothing remains unfolded. The characters, their actions and their consequences are all made transparent. Whatever be the content in a literary work, there is an appearance of it as shaped and modified and never as neutral facts. Each fact is connected to the set of other facts or events. There are no loose ends and unresolved or unshaped characters. But, in life, neither the events appear always connected to each other nor do the characters and situations stand fully resolved. In literature, on the other hand, whatever the content, it always appears as *formed* content. The "formed" nature of the content is something *created* and is in the nature of a semblance. Thus Langer points out "In outlining the action of a story, poem, or film, we habitually use the present tense, for we are not *composing* the action taken into any artistic form" (Langer 1953, p. 274). The experience like quality of narrative in literature tacitly posits a distinction between what is an experience and what only appears like an experience. The latter is a semblance or is in the realm of "virtual" as transformed by "virtual memory".

The last point needs further elaboration. Our memory is always about what is unforgettable or most significant. When we look back on our past, our memory brings together only what sticks out as relevant from out of a welter of details that can hardly be recalled. Interestingly, the remembered facts or events then get stitched together to form the fabric of life. Taken together these remembered details give us the semblance of a whole life. Quite similarly, a novel or a story is created by putting together imagined or remembered details of events, characters and situations that would bear the semblance of a whole life. The details in such a construal are so connected and relevant to one another that it stands out as an appearance of a whole lived life. As Langer puts it, "Its form is the closed, completed form that in actuality only memories have" (Langer 1953, p. 264). Two important ideas that merit attention here are as follows: (i) There is a touch of finality about the "events" in the sense that as experienced events they are unalterable; and (ii) each event appears related to the total form such that there are no irrelevant details. Yet, such is the magic of form or the manner of treatment that we here perceive them not as a more selection, but as a whole and completed life, full of rich experience. This precisely is what distinguishes the actual world of cold, isolated facts from what appears to have the wholeness of life.

The point that merits attention here is this. The domain of the aesthetic has been from discursive language which too may be regarded as a system of symbols though such a symbolic function refers to something other than itself. However, in the case of the literary arts in which the medium is always language, such a work transforms itself described as "symbol" of a kind that is self-referent in nature. This is distinguishable as an art symbol or "presentational symbol". For example, a novel or a story, though using language (discursive) as medium emerges into a unified presentational symbol (art symbol) which functions *differently*, functions as a *self- referent* symbol. This indeed is the domain of the aesthetic. As a self-referent symbol, its meaning or import cannot be separated or pulled apart from the artwork. The last point is important in the context of our discussion on the autonomous nature of the created work of art. Our understanding and appreciation of a work of art is independent of a reference to anything outside of it. This is then by way of a rejoinder to those like McAdoo who challenge the divide between art and world and life and, in that sense, challenge the autonomy thesis about it.

Aesthetic meaning or truth is self-revealing through its very inner structure. For the appreciation of such meaning, one does not have to look away from the work itself. The aesthetic structure of the work of art itself is self-revealing. Consider Bankim Chandra Chatterjee's novel *Anandamath* which was written in the backdrop of a certain sociopolitical context which is reflected in the theme of the novel. But, the aesthetic faithfully depicted in the work. To put the matter differently, a literary work (for that matter, any work of art) may have a theme which could have been borrowed from life. Yet it is the way that this theme comes across in the work that becomes the object of aesthetic appreciation and not the life incident from which it is taken or inspired by. So we may or may not the familiar with the theme as it occurs in life, which is aesthetically important is the way such a theme is developed in the work.

In support of what has been said above, Carl R. Hausman rightly points out that "at least some works of art *show* us things about the world which is outside those works. They give us insights. But they also seem capable of performing this function without being dispensable vehicles. Thus, the *extra-aesthetic consequences of some works of art are possible only in and through the intrinsic aesthetic aspect of those works*" (Housman 1986, p 164, emphasis added). So our aesthetic understanding or appreciation of a literary work of art should not be conflated with our ability to understand a certain context. For example, Van Gogh's painting *The Potato Eaters* which is about the lives of miners is aesthetically satisfying though the social condition of the miners per se is despicable. Obviously, our appreciation is for the work of art and not the theme on which it is based. So if such context-bound discursive language is imposed on a work, the aesthetic sense of the work will be completely devoured by it. The exercise that is required to be carried out is one of setting the work free from any such context while judging it aesthetically. We would argue that by actively *de*contextualizing the work, one gains a sense of freedom from any determinant context. Aesthetic enjoyment, in essence, is all about such sense of freedom. Through active participation in such a process, the individual achieves a sense of creative freedom that at once relieves one of the burdens of the so-called hard facts of life and surroundings. In this state, the individual remains in a temporary phase of selective amnesia or forgetfulness.

We are saying that whatever is statable in the discursive language will not be meaningful without the knowledge of the context. To put it slightly differently, the meaning of the discursive mode of communication depends upon the context in which it is used. Quite contrarily, the meaning of a literary work (any work of art) is contained within it and not outside of it. Viewing a work of art aesthetically involves denuding it, as it were, of its actual and possible context. Art creates a world of fiction. If we contextualize it, then it loses its fictional character and turns into a fact. On the other hand, fictionality cannot be rendered in language. It has a degree of universality that can only be felt or intuited *non*-linguistically. Facts are always specific and have their bearing in the spatio-temporal world. Fiction, on the other hand, is cut off from all bearings and for that reason not amenable to language. The point we are driving at is this. Art is not language; rather it is freedom from linguistic matrix. While attending to its fictional character, we remain in the aesthetic mode of experiencing. What is fiction is always here and now and not there and then. As soon as we start verbalizing about the fictional world, it ceases to be fictional and turns into the realm of facts.

If fictionality ceases we will be enchained by bare and unalterable facts. So it is important that the fictional character of the work of art be sustained through artistic devices. What this means is that at the time of contemplating the work of art, one must at once be *aware* of the life/art or fact/fiction divide. Experiencing art involves cutting oneself loose or detaching oneself from the context one finds oneself confronted by in everyday life. In the process the work does not remain the same physical thing but rather transforms itself into an aesthetic object. What is crucial to such experience is that the world of facts and the fictional world must never stand completely divorced from each other. Let us explain this point further. Relevant here is to mention the distinction that Tagore draws between "the world of facts" and "the world of expression".[5] Man's endeavour to survive in a hostile world involves having to discover the impersonal forces that govern the brute facts by understanding

---

[5] See Tagore (1994 impression, pp. 56–67).

the laws and principles underlying the physical world of space and time. Indeed, it is not within one's power to break, defy or ignore the laws that govern the world of facts. Thus there is a pervading sense of deficiency, finitude or limitedness one feels against the oppressively mighty impersonal world. However, man's quest for freedom from this impersonal world is deeply ingrained in human consciousness and seeks its fulfilment in our "world of expression".

Making sense of this "world of expression" is not a purely cognitive exercise. Were it so then aesthetic appreciation or understanding of a work of art would be no different from any other intellectual exercise. The view that interpreting a literary work is a cognitive exercise is fashionable among the contemporary Anglo-American critics and philosophers. Shusterman (1989, p. 6) is right in pointing out that such an approach is adopted in order to gain a sense of dignity by comparing it with the kind of activity involved in scientific and cognitive enterprise which deals only with objective truth and statable facts. What is lost sight of is that a literary text is open to multiple interpretations, and it often depends on the background from which the reader approaches it. Now it has been argued that the common assumption for underlying such exercise is that the meaning we look for in a literary work is objective or reified meaning.

But, as against this, we would want to stress here that aesthetic "meaning", quite unlike the discursively arrived meaning, is self-revealing through its inner structure. For this it is necessary to remove the debris of context-based or language-based reified meaning. The question we would raise here is as follows. Is the aesthetic value of a literary work, say a novel, based merely on our understanding of the context-based meaning, or is it something more intrinsic to it? True, we do derive some meaning on the basis of the context that is discursively provided in the work. But this alone will not be the heart or aesthetic essence of the work. Our aesthetic understanding of the novel should not be conflated with our understanding of merely a context it refers to or is based on. One would not read a novel or enjoy it if one could gain such understanding independently of the novel. For it is possible for the reader to have even a much better understanding of the context from independent sources, such as historical documents, newspapers, records, etc. than through the novel. But the aesthetic value of a novel stands on a different plane and goes beyond the meaning that is statable discursive language. The novel, as a work of art, emerges as a unified presentational symbol taking into its fold every detail that is contained in it. It is a unique structure the import of which is given to the reader in a way that cannot be stated in language.

Now in the context of literature, the notions of truth and fiction have come for a great deal of philosophical discussion in recent years. It has been argued by many thinkers that fiction adds to the value of the literary work. The fictional element in the literary work is also a way of understanding life. Julian Mitchell argues: "Fiction is a way – or it can be a way – of knowing the whole lives of people, of compressing information by compressing time" (Mitchell 1973, p. 17). He goes on to argue that "imagination is a way of perceiving…. And if we can talk about the truth and falsehood of other impressions, then we can talk of the truth and falsehood of other impressions, then we can talk of the truth and falsehood of imaginative ones, too"

(Mitchell 1973, p. 22). And, finally, he concludes, "we judge books by life and other books: we judge life by books and other life. Fiction can be as true as anything else" (Mitchell 1973) What is relevant here to understand is that fiction functions in a significant way to bring into sharp focus whole lives in a condensed form. This also is the basis for the claim for gaining a clearer understanding and insight into life situations and events. Fiction plays an important role in literature by particularizing reality with the help of details that are unreal and imaginary. In support of this view, Dilman argues that literature brings out truth about life as "the literary writer's concern … is with *the particular*, he is concerned to see things in their particularity, to capture and convey this in his work" (Dilman 1995, p. 27). It is also important to note here that such truth about life is *shown* by the work and not merely stated.

As against this, when we turn to our life experiences, we find that actions, events and characters in life are considered important or significant depending on the purpose they serve. One has a lingering awareness as to many of the events and happenings being insignificant, and the few things that do appear significant seem disconnected with or unrelated to one another. We fail to discern any structure of unity in our common experiences as we do not see any inner necessity concerning our life. Everything seems given to us provisionally or contingently.

But when we turn to art experience, on the other hand, we find that it gives us a sense of unity and necessity within it. We apprehend the inner necessity of the structure of such experience. Everything that is given in it seems unalterable and irreplaceable. So the mind grasps at what seems necessary by its very nature. The necessity we point out here does not refer to any force or compulsion outside our consciousness. Now, one might argue that in life, too, many events are felt with a sense of inalterability. But the source of such compulsion lies outside the experiencing mind. One has no control over such events. The point that is stressed here is that in our experience of art, we feel the *inner* necessity of such events that occur in a literary work of art.

A novel or a short story is marked by its unified identity which guides one to the particular details in the work. Every detail in the literary work seems relevant and related to the whole structure of the work. In aesthetic experience, we sense no compulsion from outside our consciousness; the necessity we feel here is inner in nature. And, this is germane to a sense of freedom. In short, it is the way our experience organizes itself that gives us this sense of freedom. A literary work is to be viewed in its totality and for the quality of the experience it evokes. Even though the details may be imaginary and conjured up imaginatively, the impact of the work on the reader could well be about some truth of life. It is also important to stress here that literature intensifies truth rather than taking one away from it. It also makes such truth about life more perceivable. Many commonplace aspects of life that are likely to be bypassed or ignored are brought out by the literary work in a certain perspective that makes it appear more meaningful. This enriches our experience about life. Most importantly, literary fiction performs the useful task of compressing whole lives within limits that can be grasped and reflected upon. A literary work takes us back to life and makes us see it in a new perspective. Herein lies the significance of a literary work as also its relation to life. Interestingly, our repeated interface with literary works enables us to make sense of many of the events and characters in life as we become more contemplative towards life events and situations.

References

Dilman, I. (1995, July). Art and reality: Some reflections on the arts. *Philosophical Investigations, 18*(3).

Ghosh, R. K. (1996). Notes towards understanding art/life divide. *JICPR, XIII*(3).

Hausman, C. R. (1986). *Insights in the arts*. The Journal of Aesthetics and Art Criticism.

Kivy, P. (1990). *Music alone*. Cornell University Press.

Langer, S. K. (1953). *Feeling and form*. New York: Routledge and Kegan Paul.

McAdoo, N. (1992, Spring). Can art ever be about itself. *The Journal of Aesthetics and Art Criticism, 50*(2).

Mitchell, J. (1973). Truth and fiction. In *Philosophy and the Arts: Royal Institute of Philosophical Lectures, 1971–72* (Vol. 10). Macmillan.

Mitias, M. H. (Ed.). (1986). *Possibility of aesthetic experience*. Martinus Nijhoff.

Scruton, R. (1974). *Art and imagination*. London: Methuen.

Shusterman, R. (1989). *Analytic aesthetics*. Basil Blackwell.

Tagore, R. (1994). *The religion of man*. Harper Collins impression.

Chapter 5
Metaphor and Meaning

Abstract The chapter deals with the nature and meaning of metaphor. Often a metaphor in language is "created" by breaking the rules of grammar and syntax. Thus the metaphorical meaning would be very different from the sentence meaning. It is interesting to note how metaphors are created in language and how through their overuse they become "dead metaphors". Further, the view is analysed that there is no "metaphorical meaning" but only "metaphorical use". There is also for consideration the view that metaphorical meaning is always "speaker's utterance meaning". We have argued against the position that in the case of creative metaphors, there is no literal meaning left at all, but there is left only its "metaphorical meaning". The import of it can only be experienced.

Keywords Metaphorical meaning · Metaphorical use · Speaker's intention · Non-trivial metaphor · Dead metaphor

5.1 I

Metaphors are a necessary device in all creative activity. This is true of all arts though it finds its natural home in the literary arts. Interestingly, we often refer to a visual metaphor in a derivative sense. But so wide is the use of metaphors that a proper analysis and understanding of metaphor and its meaning would be worthwhile. Metaphor has the power to convey a meaning that literal language is incapable of. The central question that we may begin with here is with regard to the nature of meaning in metaphor as it has a bearing on the problem of meaning in literature. The dichotomy of literal and metaphorical meanings gives rise to the philosophical problem concerning the relation between the two. Its parallelism to the poetic meaning as it is distinguished from the literal meaning of a poem is significant. It has been pointed out that the function of metaphor is, generally speaking, to extend the limits of language and as Henle argues that metaphors "say what cannot be said in terms of literal meanings alone" (Henle 1958, pp. 173–95). It is in this context that one distinguishes the *metaphorical* from the *literal* as applicable to words, uses of words, meanings and sentences.

Metaphors are put to diverse uses in our everyday language, such as scientific language, religious discourse, philosophical analysis and poetic language. While some of these metaphors may be shallow, banal or trivial in nature, others are often quite insightful. The sheer diversity and expansiveness of their nature tend to defy any attempt to define metaphor in terms of strict necessary and sufficient conditions. Is it possible to define metaphor? The task of defining metaphor seems a "logically vain"[1] attempt. Metaphor-making activity, like any other creative activity, is not a rule-governed activity. Creative metaphors at once bring into play an altogether new meaning or significance which could not be stated in literal language. It goes beyond the literal meaning of a linguistic statement. In other words, it evokes an idea or thought which transcends the periphery of literal meaning. In this process, we are able to see or perceive a new significance by breaking the bounds of literal language. So instead of attempting a strict definition, we may talk about the paradigmatic cases of metaphor in everyday language and in poetic language. It is important to understand how we respond to and what we look for in these cases. Undeniably, there are no strict rules for making a metaphor just as there are no strict rules for making a work of art. However, it is indeed possible to *recognize* a metaphor when we confront one. This is possible by virtue of our acquaintance with the paradigm cases. So rather than attempting a strict logical definition of metaphor, it may be a more fruitful venture to look into how the diverse kinds of metaphors function. This task may be facilitated by attending to the features that are highlighted by the various theories of metaphor.

But before we go into a fuller discussion about the nature of metaphorical meaning, our immediate concern would be the kind of metaphor we may describe as *non-trivial* or *creative* metaphor. The assumption here is that in the case of a creative metaphor, which is used in a poetic creation, the *meaning* of it is characterized by a degree of *newness* and *uniqueness*. Indeed, such a metaphor has a *fecund* form such that by a "co-creative" activity between poet and sympathetic reader, a new range of meaning or significance emerges as a flash. I would also argue that what such a metaphor does is to present or *express* the conception of an experience rather than *describe* such an experience. It would be worthwhile to say that the poetic metaphor functions as a nondiscursive or self-referent symbol as the metaphorical content or meaning remains embedded in the metaphor. It may be well to begin by asking the question, what is it like to be able to recognize a metaphor? A metaphor usually has the propositional form of the sort "X *is* Y". But how do we distinguish a metaphor from an ordinary declarative sentence since both may have the same logical form? In other words, how does one become aware that an utterance has a metaphorical content? The question we are raising here is not about how to define a metaphor but rather one of *recognizing* it when we confront it in a literary work or even in our everyday communication. Further, it is also our concern to understand how a metaphor *functions*. The assumption here is that metaphors function quite differently from how literal or ordinary language does. The use of metaphorical language is quite common in literary artworks as they add to the experiential content

---

[1] This has been argued by M. Weitz in respect of the definition of art. Please see Weitz (1956).

of the work. Integral to this is the view that the literary artworks are not primarily for cognitive understanding as the basic and primary function of art is to provide in an absorbing way a special kind of experience.

It would be worthwhile to begin by pointing to our understanding as to how natural language functions. Words are not used arbitrarily as they have determinate meanings. One must also be acquainted with the grammatical and syntactical rules of the language. Literal discourse is possible as we are able to use words according to these specifiable rules and conventions. The meaning of a literal sentence is the aggregate of the meanings of all its units, i.e. words. This is what is taken as the *literal meaning* of a sentence. In a meaningful sentence, the words used are according to the rules of grammar and syntax. Now, take the statement of the sort, "X is Y", in which the literal meanings of X and Y when put together result in incongruity or absurdity. In some such cases, the expression may turn out to be a metaphor where the metaphorical meaning is quite different even as meaning of the expression turns out to be incongruous or absurd. But one might argue that the "incongruity" or "absurdity" may be due to a grammatical lapse on the part of the utterer. A person without sufficient acquaintance with the language (say, English) may utter a sentence in which the literal meanings of the two (constituent) terms taken together may add to something incongruous or perverse. So we would ask: How do we recognize a case of metaphor? And, how do we distinguish it from a case of a malformed (or ungrammatical) sentence? In other words, how do we distinguish cases of linguistic incompetence from the cases of metaphor? Is it the case that metaphors are made by mistake?

David Novitz has the following to say in this regard, "metaphors are not made by mistake. We assume that those who coin them intend to do so, and hence that they are perfectly familiar with the literal meanings of the words that they use not-literally" (Novitz 1985, p. 103). So here an appeal is made to the intention of the language user. In other words, we intentionally make use of metaphorical language regardless of the conventional rules of grammar and syntax. We do so in order to evoke an experience of a kind that cannot be produced by using the conventional language. But the intention of the language user would be known if such usage turns out to be interesting so that it throws up some new meaning or way of looking at a situation. This will also be determined by the context in which such use is made. A metaphor does not hang loose in the air; it requires a context to be meaningful. Metaphors have a creative function like any other artwork that evokes a conception of some interesting or significant experience.

Thus the point that Novitz makes about metaphors raises the general question as to how we distinguish between a *creative* work and what has come about somewhat *accidentally*. Now one might even argue that *chance* often comes to play a role in the formation of a work of art. We would hasten to add the caveat at once that it is not the case that works of art are chancy objects or are made accidentally. It is possible to distinguish the two cases apart by an appeal to the notion of intention. A creative work is the product of conscious intentional endeavour on the part of the maker. To get back to our earlier point, a metaphorical expression is used intentionally or deliberately just as any work of art is an intentionally made *object* or *event*.

Take, for example, the utterance "The *flower* is *arrogant*". This might be a slip on the part of a person who does not have adequate competence in the English language and perhaps wanted to say that the flower is thorny or that while plucking it she was hurt by the thorn. But one can imagine a situation in which this utterance may be used as a metaphorical expression. Whether it is a case of linguistic incompetence or a metaphor depends on the context and the intention of the speaker. In a particular situation, it may intend to convey the idea that the beautiful damsel made herself unapproachable by means of her haughtiness. On the other hand, without a proper context, it may turn out to be a case of linguistic incompetence where the person wanted to communicate that while plucking the flower she got hurt by the thorn.

It would be useful to summarize the points we have discussed so far: In the first place, a metaphor arises when in a certain context it is possible for us to recognize that the language user *intended* it to be a metaphor. Secondly, the contextual evidence gets stronger when we discern that the constituent terms in the utterance *deliberately* set up a clash of literal or conventional meanings. And, this clash between the literal meanings of the two terms in the sentence gives rise to the metaphorical meaning or significance. In such a context, what is intended is quite different from what the sentence means. Further, the intended metaphorical meaning is such that it cannot be conveyed through the mere literal meaning. For example, the haughtiness of the beautiful damsel may be suggested by the way the thorn can cause us hurt. Beardsley (1958, p. 134–44) explains this clash of meanings of the two terms by treating one of the terms as the *subject* in the metaphor and the other as the *metaphorical modifier*. In the present example, "flower" is the subject and "arrogant" as the modifier. In a particular context, metaphorical modifier acquires a special sense, which then is applied to the other entity in a way that is not possible (incongruous) when it is taken in its normal sense. In our present example again, how can "arrogance" be attributed to a flower in a normal situation? But this apparent absurdity or perversity would dissolve itself into a significant experience when used metaphorically in a certain context. This results precisely because of the clash or tension between the subject and the modifier germane to such a situation.

5.2   II

We would now go on to outline the various views as to how the tension between the subject and the modifier takes place. The emotive theory maintains that like the nonsense phrase "My table is humanity turned upside down", the metaphorical expression "The flower is angry" lacks any cognitive meaning. However, the only difference that would be granted is that the latter (metaphorical expression) would be acceptable because it has somehow acquired a powerful emotive meaning. Thus it draws a distinction between the cognitive meaning that accrues in a literal or common language and the emotive meaning that comes about in a metaphorical expression. Implicit in this is that semantic truth values would not be applicable to emotive meaning. The emotive meaning is given only to one's experience. However, this theory falls short of explaining how such emotive meaning really arises.

Another theory that is generally attributed to Aristotle is that there is not much difference between a metaphor and a simile. On this view, metaphors are cases of comparison statement from which "like" or "as" has been removed, thus rendering it into an identity statement. But this theory suffers from some serious inadequacies. One might ask as to in what way such comparisons may really be significant. In a statement of the sort "X is Y", when X is compared to Y, one might ask whether the comparison is made because of degree of similarity or difference between the two. Further, if the similarity is too *close*, the comparison would seem quite banal. On the other hand, if the similarity between X and Y is *remote*, then the question would be as to what degree of remoteness. Can *any* two things be compared regardless of how remote the two are from each other? In other words, the comparison theory fails to account for the kind of tension that accrues when the *literal* meanings of the two constituent terms are pressed together. To sum up, this theory seems too *wide* to be able to account for the distinction between cases of metaphorical expression and those that are bald statement of comparison.

Interestingly, Beardsley's[2] "verbal-opposition theory" is in some ways a refined version of the theory discussed immediately before. The comparison is mediated by an iconic sign to which the modifier makes the attribution such that the comparison could be made between some feature or properties of the iconic sign and the subject in the metaphor. In the example, "The flower is shy", the modifier is attributed to a young lady who is coy and exhibits certain other features relating to the gait, posture and the colour of the cheeks and so on. The attention is focused in this case on the similarities between the features of the flower and some of the features of a shy young lady.

We would now turn to another theory that has been put forward by Max Black (1978, pp. 64–87) as "interaction view of metaphor". According to this theory, Black analyses a metaphor in terms of the two parts which he calls "the *frame* of the metaphor" and "the *focus* of the metaphor" and the interaction between the two. In our earlier example, "The flower is shy", the word "shy" is the *focus* and the term "flower" about which something is being said provides the *frame* of the metaphor. Both frame and focus evoke certain "thoughts" or conceptions, which then *interact* so as to result in a *new* meaning, which was not there in either of the two terms. Further, according to Black, the frame affects an *extension* of meaning to the focal word "shy". On this view, a metaphorical statement has two constituents, namely, the frame and the focus (or the principal subject and the subsidiary subject), each standing for *a system of associated commonplaces*. The example Black uses is "Man is a wolf" and points out that the literal meaning of the word "wolf" may be understood in terms of commonplace beliefs that are associated with wolves, say the traits of being carnivorous, fierce, treacherous, etc. Now, the effect of this subsidiary subject is to give explanation to the meaning of the principal subject. Or, in

---

[2] For a clear exposition of the theory, see Callaway (1986, pp. 73–88).

other words, the principal subject is "seen through" the *filter* of the subsidiary subject while itself influencing the implicative predication.

This theory also helps us understand the distinction between trivial and nontrivial metaphors. According to Max Black, only non-trivial metaphors can be explained by the "interaction view", as trivial metaphors are more amenable to the comparison or substitution thesis. Christopher Backe (1980, pp. 1985–93), on the other hand, argues that all metaphors, trivial and non-trivial, can be explained by the "interaction theory" by modifying the theory. This could be done by an appeal to the notion of "entrenchment". For him, trivial metaphors, like non-trivial metaphors, are also interactionist. But the trivial metaphor, through its repeated use and consequent familiarity, becomes so entrenched in the literal discourse that the process of interaction is short-circuited. This renders the metaphor emaciated, for the process of interaction is no more apparent. The trivial metaphor behaves much the same way as an ordinary word and its literal meaning. It is important to note that the presence or absence of epistemic creativity of a metaphor is not based on any difference in the metaphor's operational logic. Through overmuch familiarity a metaphor becomes so entrenched in the literal discourse that the interactive process gets aborted so as to destroy its creativity. Overmuch familiarity with the use of a metaphor takes away its fecundity and renders it into a "dead" metaphor.

5.3   III

Having briefly made a survey of the various theories about how metaphors function, let us now turn to an analysis of the nature of its *meaning*. Such a concern of the philosopher is prompted by a desire to relate it to a general theory of meaning. To put the matter in a perspective, metaphorical meaning poses a challenge in respect of its having to be incorporated into a general theory of meaning. One might suggest in a general way that metaphorical meaning of an expression or sentence arises in spite of and in deviance from what is asserted in the literal sense. For example, the sentence "John is a pig" conveys *not* what it asserts in terms of its semantic and syntactical structure; its metaphorical sense is that John is greedy, obstinate and so on. The speaker of such a sentence does not really mean that John is a pig. Through common and frequent use of such a sentence, its literal sense ceases to be, and one spontaneously takes it to mean that John is a greedy person. Here, does it make good sense to draw a distinction between the literal meaning and the metaphorical meaning? It is obvious that the only meaning that is available here is the metaphorical meaning and there is no literal meaning worth considering. But difficulty arises when such expressions are treated as "dead metaphors" implying thereby that there is hardly any warrant for treating such meaning as metaphorical meaning. We have already denied such "dead" metaphors of having any literal meaning since that would be an absurdity. At the same time, we deny legitimacy to retain its metaphorical meaning. So how do we understand the nature of metaphorical meaning?

In this connection, it would be useful to consider the views of Davidson (1984). According to him the only meaning that there is is the literal meaning, which is "used" metaphorically. He holds the view that there is no such thing as *metaphorical meaning*. We might ask: If there is only metaphorical use and no such thing as metaphorical meaning, then can every word be used metaphorically? Further, how do we distinguish between literal meaning and metaphorical meaning? Davidson seems to be arguing that a sentence has only literal meaning but is used to communicate something metaphorically. Let us illustrate the point. In our example "Man is a wolf", the only meaning it has, according to Davidson, is its literal meaning though it is being used as a metaphor. But, then, how do we account for what it conveys metaphorically? In this respect, "Dead metaphors" pose a challenge in so far as such metaphors do not seem to have any literal meaning besides what they convey metaphorically. One might argue that such metaphors lend weight to the theory that there is no such thing as metaphorical meaning. Through constant and repeated use of such metaphorical expression, such expressions lose their literal meaning altogether. But Davidson (1984, p. 245) and many others refuse to accept them as metaphors at all, because through usage the meaning they come to convey can be treated as no other than the literal meaning. This point will come for fuller discussion a little later. In the case of other creative metaphors, the argument is that what they assert in the literal sense is *used* to convey what goes in the name of metaphorical meaning. But rejoinder to this position is that the literal meaning or sense in such metaphorical expressions is a mere absurdity or perversity. But as a metaphorical expression, we are able to understand it in a more transparent and significant way. So we would join issue with Davidson in holding legitimacy for metaphorical meaning. The wider issue here is that understanding metaphorical meaning is not premised on a cognitive judgement through semantic truth values.

Let us now turn to David Cooper who brings out this point by considering how a possible definition of metaphorical utterance fails to meet the condition of being necessary and sufficient. The definition he considers is as follows. "(X) Someone utters S metaphorically if and only if he says that P, but without intending to convey a belief that P" (Cooper 1986, pp. 112–13). Cooper goes on to ask if (X) states a necessary and sufficient condition of metaphorical utterance. According to him, it cannot be treated as necessary condition because "there seem to be utterances, of so called 'dead' metaphors, which have established meanings besides their literal ones – so that speakers of them can be at once talking metaphorically and expressing the belief which the utterances, in their secondary meanings, can express. Hence it is not necessary for the metaphoricity of an utterance of S that the speaker does not intend to convey the belief that P. (For S and P substitute 'John is a pig' and 'John is greedy') Now we know how many writers, including Davidson, would react to this point: they would deny that the utterances in question are really, metaphorical. 'Dead' metaphors, they say, are not metaphors" (Cooper 1986, p. 112).

It must be noted that deviance by itself does not allow us to construe the utterances as metaphorical. "Suppose someone says '3+79=94', ...knowing that it is false and that his audience recognizes that he knows this, we seem forced by (X) to say that he was speaking metaphorically. The trouble is it is difficult to make sense of the idea that it could be metaphorical" (Cooper 1986, p. 115). The two points that we have tried to focus on are as follows. (i) In the case of metaphors that have been used for long, the only meaning the speaker wants to convey is the metaphorical sense as there is no other literal meaning that such a sentence conveys. In other words, there is no dichotomy between what the speaker intends to convey and what the sentence conveys in a routine way, the two are no two different things. So the criticism that the speaker says something and does not intend to convey what he says does not apply to "dead" metaphors. If, on the other hand, the criterion is taken to be a necessary condition of metaphorical utterance, then "dead" metaphors will not be acceptable as metaphor at all. (ii) The other point is that just because a sentence/utterance is deviant or seemingly meaningless, it does not follow that such an utterance is a metaphorical utterance. Not all grammatically ill-formed sentences can claim to be metaphors.

When we critically consider the notion of literal meaning, the alleged divide between literal meaning and metaphorical meaning seems to blur out. This is indeed interesting since the literal meaning of a word represents only how the word has come to be used in the past. For sure, the standard dictionary provides only an account of it as to the sense in which the members of a linguistic community have used it. For that matter, it also sometimes records a shift in the sense over a period of time or across the linguistic community. For example, recently, in the wake of an attack on the W.T.C. in Manhattan, the president George W. Bush used the expression "Crusade against terrorism" in which the word "Crusade" was purportedly used *not* in the sense in which it stood for religious wars in the middle ages. There has been a shift in the meaning of the term over the ages as it now stands for a concerted campaign in the cause of some laudable objective.

The point, however, is that even the so-called literal meaning of a word is not something static, rigidly fixed and unchanging. It only stands for the common consensus of a majority of the members of a linguistic community who use the word in a particular sense in a particular context. On the other hand, a metaphorical utterance, after repeated use over a period of time, stands for a sense, which then forms the part of the core meaning of the word or expression used therein. Thus, the word "pig" when used in utterances like "John is a pig" has as part of its core meaning the sense of being greedy. What may appear at first "deviant" meaning (in the case of a fresh metaphor) through use over a long period of time gets assimilated to its core meaning. This account of meaning is tellingly borne out by what are known as "dead" metaphors.

For those traditionalist thinkers who regard metaphorical meaning as what belongs to the metaphorical utterance, the word "pig" means as much a kind of animal as it means greediness. And so, "John is a pig" means "John is greedy", for the word "pig" now stands also for a person who is greedy. Now there are at least two possible ways in which one may argue against such a position and thus strike down the thesis that metaphorical meaning belongs to such utterances. One argument would be the following. Suppose that I point to an animal and say to my little daughter, "Over there, that is a pig". Here, I do not necessarily mean that she should regard the animal at the same time as a greedy creature or that whenever she sights such an animal, she should say that the animal she confronts is a greedy creature. Again, when I point to a picture and say to a nursery class "This is a pig", all that I mean to convey to the class is that the animal in the chart is called "pig" and not, say, "goat". But when I point to John and whisper into the ears of my close friend "He is a pig", my friend will understand what I mean, maybe after satisfying himself that I am not suffering from the effects of some hangover after the last nights drinking bout.

The defender of the traditional thesis might retort that the examples cited above only go to demonstrate the indeterminacy of meaning and that the word (in this case, pig) may be used in two different senses depending on the context. Further, this is true of many other words (nonmetaphorical) and their usage. For example, the words "sole", "plane", "class", "bachelor", etc. can be used in different senses without conveying any metaphorical meaning. So, in this regard, the word "pig" behaves in no significantly different way from the other common words. Just as the word "sole" can be used in the sense of "only/single" as well as what belongs to my shoes, the word "pig" also has two different senses—"animal of a kind" and "greedy creature". In short, the argument would be that metaphorical meaning belongs as much to a word or sentence as does the so-called literal meaning.

The opponent may counter the argument by pointing out that this is to beg the question as to whether "John is a pig" means "John is greedy" is really an instance of metaphorical meaning as this is part of the established linguistic practice to use the two expressions as equivalent if not identical. This brings us to the central point of the opponent's argument.

The argument would be on the following lines. The opponent refutes any such claim of the traditionalist to treat meaning of "dead" metaphors as metaphorical meaning, for "dead" metaphors are not metaphors at all. If the meaning of a "dead" metaphor behaves almost like literal meaning, it is because it can no longer be treated as a metaphor. The point is that in the case of non-trivial, creative or fresh metaphors, the meaning does not belong to the metaphorical sentence or utterance; it is identifiable with the *intention* of the speaker (or user of the metaphorical utterance). John Searle most prominently represents this view. According to him, "metaphorical meaning is always speaker's utterance meaning" (Searle 1980, p. 93) This way of looking at metaphorical meaning opens out scope for its interpretation by the hearer/reader. Not only will the speaker claim one or the other actual intention as the metaphorical meaning, even the hearer could interpret in terms of *possible* intended meaning. As David Cooper elaborates the Searlean position: "A sentence's (literal) meaning... is that which, in conjunction with certain background assumptions, determines the conditions under which it is true or false. A speaker's meaning, on the other hand, is a function of his intentions, so that talking about a metaphor's possible meaning is 'talking about possible speaker's intentions'" (Cooper 1986, p. 67). Since the speaker's actual intention may not be known, the hearer may interpret the metaphorical expression or utterance regardless of such knowledge so long as the interpretation seems plausible as some possible speaker's intention. Such an approach makes way for the indeterminacy of meaning. Thus Cooper rightly argues: "There is no way to reconcile the fact of indeterminacy with the idea of metaphorical meanings as speakers' intended propositions" (Cooper 1986, p. 70). However, we would rejoin by saying the speaker's intention, given a specific context, becomes transparent for anyone to understand its import. In other words, we would put forward the argument that it would be a "fallacy" to look for the intention of the speaker anywhere other than in the utterance as it is given in the context. For example, in a diplomatic exchange of communications if one of the party says "The ball is in your court", it would naturally mean that the other party is required or expected to take some desired step. Nobody would take it to mean literally that the tennis ball has been actually thrown to the opponent. The intention of the speaker in such a context is transparently clear. So, in such cases where is the question of meaning indeterminacy. The point we are making is that in the case of metaphorical use of a sentence, the context makes the intention of the speaker as to its metaphorical meaning. Searle's point about the intention of the speaker constituting meaning of a metaphorical utterance is well taken, but how does it become open to the charge of indeterminacy or perversity? The intention of the speaker in using metaphorical utterance becomes transparent in relation to the context or situation in which this occurs.

The purported difficulty as indicated by David Cooper earlier with regard to the Searlean position is that of having to explain why metaphorical utterances should not be treated as "perverse". If the speaker has some intention that he does not consciously allow his utterance to convey, then the so-called metaphorical sentence he utters would seem to represent only a perversity. Perhaps a possible alternative to such a view would be that what the speaker intends to convey cannot be done by the use of discursive (literal) language. Thus while Searle is critical of the traditional view that metaphorical meaning belongs to the utterance or sentence on the basis of the argument that its distinction from literal meaning cannot be clearly identified, his own view seems to run into rough weather as it remains vulnerable to the possible accusation of perversity and the charge of indeterminacy. But as we have argued, such a charge can be met by holding the view that the intention of the speaker would be quite transparent with reference to the context or situation in which it is being used.

5.4   IV

Donald Davidson adopts a more radical approach. He rejects the very notion of metaphorical meaning. In his paper "What metaphors mean" he categorically states, "metaphors mean what the words, in their most literal interpretation, mean, and nothing more"[16]. Rejecting the notion of "metaphorical meaning", Davidson argues that a metaphor does not have a special "cognitive content" other than its literal meaning. Underlying such a position is the distinction Davidson draws "between what words mean and what they are used to do". And for him "metaphor belongs exclusively to the domain of use. It is something brought off by the imaginative employment of words and sentences and depends entirely on the ordinary meanings of those words and hence on the ordinary meanings of the sentences they comprise"

(Davidson 1984, p. 245). In a metaphorical sentence, the ordinary meanings of the words employed in it do not cease to be operative. Only because the ordinary meanings in a sentence remain in force that one creatively *uses* it as a metaphor. It follows that metaphorical use will not be possible without the ordinary literal meanings of words. So, for Davidson, there is no metaphorical meaning as there is only metaphorical use.

As against the position outlined above, we may raise the following two critical points: (a) What does Davidson really mean by "ordinary literal" meaning of words? And (b) how such literal meaning of words is related to literal meaning of sentences? On the ground that every word that is used in a sentence must have a "literal" meaning, does it follow that the *sentence* so formed must also have a "literal" meaning? Those who argue in support of the concept of metaphorical meaning precisely object to the thesis that the *sentence* so formed with words that have literal meaning can only have literal meaning and nothing else. The point is that a sentence in which the words have literal meaning may give rise to metaphorical meaning besides conveying its literal meaning, if there is any such meaning at all. What the metaphor means is not the same as its literal meaning. The supporter of metaphorical meaning can thus turn the table on the Davidsonian approach by claiming that in the case of metaphorical sentences, the words *combine* in a way such that the sentence is associated with *metaphorical* meaning. In other words, the literal meaning gets transformed into metaphorical meaning; it no longer remains the literal meaning. Interestingly, the words in such a sentence will continue to have their literal meanings though what may emerge by the combination of these words would be metaphorical meaning. Such a metaphorical sentence ceases to have any literal meaning as it would turn out to be incongruous or a perversity. In the sentence "John is a pig", its literal meaning based on the literal meaning of "John" (the name of the person) and its conjunction with the literal meaning "pig" (and animal) would be perverse, and so we turn to its metaphorical meaning which is incapable of being described in literal sense.

So, in a metaphorical sentence, the word that originally had a "literal/ordinary" meaning now comes to acquire a metaphorical meaning or signification. In the sentence "John is a pig", the word "pig" no longer has the ordinary meaning, but in conjunction with the other constituents in the sentence acquires the metaphorical meaning that it now has. Josef Stern rightly asks us to "note that Davidson shifts from talking of the ordinary literal meaning of the *words* that occur in a metaphor to that of the *sentences* that comprise those words" (Stern 2000, p. 47). And he then argues: "It is clear... that a metaphorical use depends on the literal meaning of the *word*(s) so used, but it is not nearly as clear that it depends on the literal meaning of the *sentence* comprised by those words" (Stern 2000) The distinction between talk about the literal meaning of words from talk about purported literal meaning of the sentence is crucial in as much as in a metaphorical sentence there is no literal meaning at all. All there is in it is its metaphorical meaning. For example, in the sentence "Juliet is the sun" (or "John is a pig"), each of the individual words may have their literal meaning. But does the sentence as a whole have a literal meaning? Rather, it might be argued that such a sentence (metaphor) *ceases* to have any literal meaning.

If we go along with Davidson and stress on the literal meaning of a metaphorical sentence, we land up in the absurdity of looking for the truth conditions by which such sentence could be known as true (even though we know it to be absurdly false). In other words, since we cannot set down the truth conditions for such sentences, there would be no literal *meaning* as it should be understood within the Davidsonian framework of meaning which must always be based on its truth conditions. Davidson's position that there is no metaphorical meaning as instead there is only metaphorical *use* lands one into a paradoxical claim that the metaphorical sentence has a *literal* meaning which is not amenable to any truth conditions.

Let us put the point into perspective. This opposition to Davidson's thesis against the notion of metaphorical meaning squarely rests on his explanation that metaphorical *use* of a sentence depends upon its *literal* meaning. The opponent argues that there is no such thing as the literal meaning of a *metaphorical* sentence. Only words in the sentence can be said to have literal meaning. One must draw here a distinction between literal meaning of a word in a sentence and the meaning of a sentence. In the case of a metaphorical sentence, what accrues is its metaphorical meaning. There is no literal meaning of a metaphorical sentence. R.M. White has summed up this objection to Davidson's thesis more pointedly. "The ordinary, literal, sense of a metaphorical sentence, if such exists, *never* plays a role in the apprehension of that metaphor when we are apprehending it *as* metaphor. To apprehend a metaphor *as* a metaphor involves ignoring whatever literal sense it may have" (White 1996, p. 226). White is quite right in maintaining that there is no use for the literal meaning of a metaphorical sentence even if it be assumed that there is such meaning. For example, what literal meaning do we attach to the metaphorical sentence "John is a pig", since the only meaning that we attribute to it is metaphorical meaning. And, there is no use for semantic truth value for metaphorical meaning.

From the foregoing discussion, we may thus conclude that the notion of metaphorical meaning is not amenable to a strict semantic theory. In the case of a creative metaphor, the meaning that it conveys is not even paraphrasable. What such a metaphor seems to do is not merely say *about* something but rather to *show* it. To put it a little differently, a metaphor makes us see a state of affairs at once and vividly such that the same cannot be described in a semantically literal sentence. Meaning or significance of metaphor, like that of a work of art, remains embedded in the metaphorical utterance and cannot be separated apart from it. This is what makes it difficult to fit metaphorical meaning into a formal theory of semantics.

We would point out that metaphorical meaning may thus be regarded as of the nature of a "presentational symbol" in the sense in which Susanne Langer (1953) speaks of an art symbol. Indeed, she distinguishes such a symbol from a "discursive symbol". Literal language, for example, stands for a system of "discursive symbols" in which every word functions as such a symbol. Each word has a designated meaning and so words in a literal sentence add up to a designated meaning by the same logic. But the relation between word and its meaning, or sentence and its meaning, is contingent. For this reason, the same meaning may be given out by another set of words or a sentence made up of such words. The underlying point here is that meaning of a discursive system of symbols (a literal sentence) can be conveyed by another set of symbols (a sentence), the latter standing in a definite and determinate relation to its meaning such that the two can be separated apart. But in the case of a metaphor or metaphorical sentence, its meaning or import cannot be pulled apart from it. A metaphor has a unique meaning which cannot be replaced by another sentence. It is in this context that we would suggest that the "interaction view" comes closest to accounting for our way of looking upon metaphorical meaning as a nondiscursive or presentational symbol much as a poem (or an artwork) may be so regarded. As Langer maintains, a nondiscursive symbol is a unified whole the meaning or "import" of which cannot be pulled apart from it. The symbol and its import are given as fused together and to intuit the symbol is to apprehend its import as well. This self-*referent* nature of the symbol enables one to apprehend its meaning with an "immediacy" which is characteristic of artistic intuition. To put the matter a little differently, an art symbol does not function as a *surrogate* for something other than itself. For such a symbol, there is no other; it is what it is. It follows that the meaning of a metaphor (poetic) is in the nature of an experience or insight. Carl Hausman points out that such meaning is both "unique" and "extra linguistic". As he puts it, "A metaphorical expression functions so that it is creative of its significance, thus providing new insight, through designating a unique, extra linguistic and extra-conceptual referent that had no place in the intelligible world before the metaphor was articulated" (Hausman 1983, p. 186). Elsewhere, he has argued, "that metaphors create integrated wholes that generate more than linguistic items and are something more than conceptual perspectives" (Hausman 1991, p. 45). It may be noted that the position taken here presupposes unparaphrasability thesis, which is crucial to Black's view.

A point that follows from the position stated above is that a metaphor is non-assertoric expression of experience. No truth value can be attributed to the metaphor as it does not state a fact or a factual position. As Stephen Davies puts it, the metaphor maker aims not at asserting belief but at conveying an experience to the audience. "The metaphor is the *expression* rather than a description, of an experience" (Davies 1984, pp. 197–8). The attribution of truth value is possible only to the literal or propositional content of the metaphor. But the meaning we are claiming for a metaphor transcends the literal content. Its meaning consists in its ability to make us *see* the significance or import of what is presented. A metaphor functions as nondiscursive or presentational symbol as it is made clear by Susanne K. Langer (1953). The metaphor and its meaning are conjoined together in a way that the word and its meaning are not. Metaphorical meaning stands for a realm of experience which we directly apprehend without mediation of the meaning units of the words in it. Once the metaphorical meaning is apprehended, the literal meaning of the metaphorical sentence is left behind as contingent and uninteresting. What is important to note here is the tension that is set up by the literal and the metaphorical meanings. In the case of "dead metaphors", the tension is completely lost through its repeated overuse.

The central point of our discussion has been the nature and status of metaphorical meaning. The identification of metaphorical meaning with the intention of the speaker as stated by Searle is based on the distinction he draws between literal meaning and metaphorical meaning. For him, literal meaning belongs to the sentence or utterance, while metaphorical meaning is what belongs to the intention of the speaker. But it leaves the view to the criticism made by David Cooper that intention of the speaker being in the mind of the speaker would suffer from indeterminacy. However, as against this we have argued that the charge of indeterminacy or perversity of meaning would not be valid as the speaker's meaning would be quite transparent in relation to a particular situation and context. A more radical view is that of Davidson for whom there is only literal meaning and this is only used metaphorically. In other words, there is only metaphorical *use* and no metaphorical meaning. We have argued against this position that in the case of non-trivial or creative metaphorical expression there is no literal meaning left at all. The only meaning that there is is its metaphorical meaning.

References

Backe, C. (1980, Winter). Towards a unified theory of metaphor. *The Journal of Aesthetics and Art Criticism.*
Beardsley, M. C. (1958). *Aesthetics: Problems in the philosophy of criticism.* Brace & Court Inc.: Harcourt.
Black, M. (1978). Metaphor. In J. Margolis (Ed.), *Philosophy looks at the arts.* Philadelphia: Temple University Press.
Callaway, H. G. (1986). Beardsley on metaphor. In L. Aagaard-Mogensen & L. De Vos (Eds.), *Text, literature, and aesthetics.* Amsterdam: Rodopic.
Cooper, D. (1986). *Metaphor.* Blackwell.
Davidson, D. (1984). What metaphors mean. In *Inquiries into truth and interpretation.* Oxford: Clarendon.
Davies, S. (1984, Spring). Truth values and metaphors. *The Journal of Aesthetics and Art Criticism.*
Hausman, C. (1983, Winter). Metaphors, referents, and individuality. *The Journal of Aesthetics and Art Criticism.*
Hausman, C. (1991). *Metaphor and art.* Cambridge, MA: Cambridge University Press.
Henle, P. (Ed.). (1958). Metaphor. In *Language, thought, and culture.* University of Michigan Press.
Langer, S. K. (1953). *Feeling and form.* New York: Routledge and Kegan Paul.
Novitz, D. (1985). *Metaphor, derrida, and davidson.* Winter: The Journal of Aesthetics and Art Criticism.
Searle, J. (1980). Metaphor. In A. Ortony (Ed.), *Metaphor and thought.* Cambridge, MA: Cambridge University Press.
Stern, J. (2000). *Metaphor in context.* New York: MIT.
Weitz, M. (1956). *The role of theory in aesthetics.* The Journal of Aesthetics and Art Criticism.
White, R. M. (1996). *The structure of metaphor.* New York: Blackwell.

Chapter 6
The Literary Narrative and Moral Values

Abstract The chapter deals with narrative identity as it is created both in life and in literary work. It is very much the case that our personal identities in life are created by means of narrative wherein one puts together selectively favourable traits of character in an imaginative construal. Selectivity and connectedness of elements are the hallmark of such construal. This goes for the literary work as well which is characterized by a "closed form" and causal interconnectedness among the elements such as personal traits, events and circumstances. The thesis that art making is no different from creating one's own or other's identity by means of narrative construction provides an interesting insight into the creative process. A critical appreciation of a literary work does not allow the reader to remain untouched by the moral and ethical dimensions of the narrative. We argue, however, that the moral knowledge that one may glean out from the literary work is only a by-product and does not claim to be in the nature of the essence of the creative work. Aesthetic experience of the literary work must supervene over any such moral or social message.

Keywords Narrative identity · Closed form · Moral message · Anti-essentialism · Autonomy thesis

6.1 I

A narrative work of art has an interesting way of working itself out. In a work of fiction, the author creates identities of characters as they are related to different life situations. How does one go about it? What kind of exercise is this? Indeed, the process seems quite similar to the way one creates one's own self-identity in terms of a narrative. Such process is undertaken both for oneself as well as for projecting one's identity to others. The thesis that art making is, in essence, no different from creating one's own (or that of other's) identity by means of narrative construction provides an interesting insight into the creative process.

Let us begin with the case of self-identity. From out of a welter of details relating to one's various activities, pursuits, achievements, failures and various other incidents and experiences, only a few significant details are selected such that these

R. K. Ghosh, *Essays in Literary Aesthetics*, SpringerBriefs in Philosophy,
https://doi.org/10.1007/978-981-13-2460-4_6

would show the individual in a favourable light. Those that would show the individual in a poor light would be excluded from such a construal. The underlying point is that the individual's self-identity is made up in terms of a narrative construal. In other words, there remains the possibility of making alternative construals depending on the way the individual would want to believe what his self-identity is. The same process would apply when a person wants to project oneself to others in a particular way. Thus there can be multiple narrative identities of the same person depending on the choice of particular traits, events, responses, etc. that one may choose to highlight. There is creativity involved in such processes.

It is interesting to note here that according to Novitz, we construct our individual identities by means of telling stories about ourselves "much the way that works of art are produced" (Novitz 1989, p. 57). Such narratives, far from being mere flat chronicle of events, have a coherent and unified structure with a definite focus. And, as in a literary narrative, it does not matter whether the "facts" incorporated in it are true or imagined so it is the case with the narrative identity of the individual self so long as the emergent structure is *coherent* and *unified*. One might well imagine that nobody wants to be seen by others as a mean, nasty, venomous character who is a failure in life. So the "choice" of facts and/or inclusion of imagined details would naturally be built into the narrative structure. The important point to note here is that in either process, facts or events that are considered "inessential" to the created structure are left out. What is included in a work of art or a narrative identity must appear to be necessary and relevant for the whole structure; the inessential has no place in it. The construal is of its essence. The identity of a person is thus reduced to a mere narrative construal that is based on facts, traits, events, situations and responses regardless of whether these are facts or fictional.

It is pertinent to ask here as to why does one construct one's identity in a certain way. What might be the intention or motivation for doing so? Now, it has been argued that narrative identity is constructed for the reason that we have a "moral interest" as to what sort of person we are or want to be and that " how we view and think of ourselves influences our behaviour" (Novitz 1989, p. 60). For example, if one finds it possible to invent or construct a narrative structure which would support the conviction that as an individual the person has in the past acted courageously, then such a person would also tend to be bold and courageous in all his *future* dealings. The narrative identity guides, to a large extent, our future actions and plans. From out of a range of different *possible* structures, only the one that may be helpful at a particular point of time would be selected. In other words, a narrative identity will tend to have a certain degree of fecundity in as much as it is likely to condition our actions and behaviour in the future. Thus:

> Our narrative identities are neither God-given nor innate, but are painstakingly acquired as we grow, develop, and interact with the people around us. Our identities may, of course, be based on past experience, but such experience, we have seen, is too complicated, amorphous and anomalous (even if accurately recalled) to admit of a coherent self-image. Most often, I have stressed, life-narratives, and the identities to which they give rise, are *imaginative construal* which people adopt, and in terms of which they select and order past events in their lives (Novitz 1989, p. 65, emphases added).

What follows from this account is that such "imaginative construals" are open to emendations. Thus one enjoys a certain amount of freedom in the matter of making an imaginative construal, which will go for one's own personal identity or that for another person. Also important here to note is that it is not always the case that the individual *chooses* an identity for himself. "At times our identities are given to us, and we become the beneficiaries, victims, or playthings of the narrative that others create and push in our direction" (Novitz 1989, p. 69). This is quite often the case with political leaders and public figures. Often we pull out a few details from their life in public domain and make a construal on that basis and thrust it on the individual. For example, often the elections are fought and won and lost on the basis of such narrative construal made by the public and thrust upon the political leader. Popularity or otherwise of a public figure would depend largely on the narrative identity thrust upon the person by others. Take, for instance, the recent case about how a powerful media mogul's wife (equally well known as a media controller) strangled her own daughter to death. Around this skeletal fact, competing narrative identities have been built around all the three principle characters showing one or the other in a way that keeps shifting blame from one to another or to both parents. Narrative identities are being built by picking out details from the past life, marriages and relationships. Similarly, a political greenhorn riding on the wave of a well-crafted narrative identity swept the assembly elections and became the Chief Minister of a state though his later actions and responses completely belied the narrative. Clearly, a distinction can be drawn between acceptability of a narrative identity and its truth; the narrative identity that is acceptable may not be the true identity of the person. Acceptability is a matter of preference, which indeed is quite complex in a given social situation. Suffice it to note here that narrative identities are fictional in character as they are products of imagination.

Note that Novitz entertains here the following three different possibilities. First, for whatever reasons, some people may not succeed in constructing narrative identities for themselves and so may have to live through life with a *fractured* self, as it were. Second, the individual might be able to construct for himself a narrative identity with at least some degree of *free* choice. Third, others may impose the narrative identity on the individual and create and push such identity in his direction. The implications of the third possibility are grave as it has social and political ramifications. By and large, it would be *social acceptability* for certain kinds of identities that would guide or goad people into adopting and preferring some identity structures over others. Political propaganda and media fabrication have often been used for the purposes of swaying the public opinion on issues of vital importance. The process, as Novitz puts it, is " quintessentially political" (Novitz 1989, p. 67) since "[i]t is the social acceptability of a narrative identity, and not the *truth* of the narrative that constitutes it, that determines what we regard as natural, worthy, or excellent in human behaviour" (Novitz 1989, p. 70). It is common knowledge that a free media plays around with such alternative narrative structures about public figures and political personalities. Who would deny that what we "know" about cine stars and other celebrities in different walks of life is what we are told in terms of the narrative construal put out by the media and related sources.

Let us now turn to some interesting parallelisms between the process of constructing narrative identities and that of making works of art. Both are marked by
the principle of selectivity, imaginative linkages and a certain special focus in order
to give the product a unified structure. The *literary* narrative as much as the narrative *personhood* is fashioned out by organizing the details on a timescale in a way
that the emergent "narrative time" turns out to be different from time in real life.
This enables the narrative structure to acquire a particular slant or focus on some
distinctively preferred value or norm. Further, the social acceptability of works of
art and narrative identities depends on their conformability to a set of prevailing
values. Thus it has been argued by Novitz that "political dynamism and intrigue"
come to play a definitive role in criticism of works of art as well as that of people
and their ideas. In other words, the state may develop a vested interest in nurturing
and highlighting certain narrative identities or personhood just as it may want to
encourage certain kinds of artistic creations.

What we are arguing is that personal identities are quite like works of art: they
are made in the same way, they come to be treated by society in the like manner, and
they come to be accepted or rejected on similar grounds. In the ultimate analysis,
Novitz suggests, it is the State that develops a vested interest in encouraging and
perpetuating certain kinds of personal identities and works of art. On this view, the
sense of personhood one acquires by the use of the narrative is based on its social
acceptability.

Some of the major points in Novitz's thesis may be brought out here by way of a
brief critical appraisal of the matter. It is indeed an interesting point that we develop
and acquire a sense of personhood by telling stories about us. That a distinction
should be drawn between such narratives and mere chronicle of events in one's life
seems quite well taken. The stories that we tell about ourselves are usually carefully
crafted so as to project a special *focus* on some aspect of our personhood. Certain
common tendencies are discernible towards this end. For example, we would generally want to be "seen" as courageous rather than diffident in matters where we are
required to take certain decisions, or as generous rather than mean in our dealings
with other people, and so on. And so, while constructing a narrative about ourselves,
we would so arrange the sequences or twist and turn the events in a way that the
emergent structure bears out our claim (even if implicitly held) to certain preferred
virtues. It follows that for telling a "story" about ourselves (i.e. a narrative), (a) we
may *selectively* pick on some details, events and situations, (b) interpolate some of
the elements that may be based on imagination and (c) put them all together in a
sequence and manner that would give the structure a *closure* and *finality*. Novitz
holds the view that (a), (b) and (c) are identical to what goes on and into creating a
literary or visual work of art and that works of art and narrative identities are created
almost in the same manner and for the purposes that are quite similar. However, we
would contend here that the basic purpose and motivation for creating works of art
are essentially *aesthetic* in character while those for constructing narrative identities
are mainly *moral*.

We would now turn to a critical point of some importance. True, the stories we
tell about ourselves are nearly always for *others* in order to project a self-image to

them. While we may agree what Novitz believes it to be the case about narrative identities, we do not agree with it wholly. In our view, the individual also has an implicit awareness (or understanding) of his own personhood quite *apart* from the narratives he constructs for others. Awareness of one's own sense of identity is based on actual memory of life experiences in the past. The traditional view of self equates personal identity with the continuity of memory so that we are able to think of ourselves as being "ourselves" at different points of time and place. Of course, the memory may tend to be selective though this does not preclude the possibility of carrying in one's memory both pleasant *and* unpleasant experiences. Our failings and failures are known *to us* far too well even for all our attempts to reconstruct them differently *for others*. Novitz does not seem to take into consideration this important point. In other words, there is a sense of selfhood that we create for ourselves as we recall to the mind the past events of our life. Perhaps the term "create" in this context is inappropriate, for the process only involves some past life experiences being given to the mind as our memory recalls them *selectively*, though. Were it not so, the individual would not be given to moral reflections.

Let us again go back to the point that we *do* tell stories about ourselves to others. It is not the case that these stories have always a full-blown character. We tend to talk about our own actions and responses to situation from a particular perspective. Even when we do construct such narratives, it seems possible to do so only *because* we already have an implicit awareness about our own personhood of whatever kind. It is not merely the case that by telling stories about ourselves, we create our identities. Rather construction of such narratives *can* be possible only because we have a pre-existent sense of personhood. Recourse to narrative process may be taken when we want to convey to others an image or identity of ours that is *different* from the one we have for ourselves. Narrative identities, even if they be granted as what we are able to construct freely, are only symptomatic of our being already in possession of an intimate sense of selfhood. Novitz seems to take the very symptom of selfhood as what *constitutes* it.

But we would argue that we are *able* to tell stories about ourselves *because* we have an awareness of selfhood. Thus it would be quite useful to draw a distinction between narrative identities that the individual may create (mainly, for others) on the one hand and his *own* pervading sense of selfhood on the other hand. If this distinction is not made, then Novitz's attempt to delineate different narrative identities would only lapse into the Humean quandary. Multiple narrative structures can exist in a social space if only they belong to some*one*; or else, they would fall outside of the parameters of communicative strategies. One can talk about oneself because one has a sense of *identity*. Novitz's suggestion about narrative identities, on our view, must be taken in this perspective. We construct narrative identities for ourselves mainly for presenting or projecting our self-image *to others*. We want others to judge and evaluate our personality favourably. We want them to view or review our actions and responses in the context we provide to them by means of narrative identities. We want to seek others' support and endorsement for our behaviour pattern in general as also for certain specific actions/responses, in particular. Thus the purpose for which we tell stories about ourselves is mainly to get others to see our actions with a sense of *moral* approval. And if such exercise comes through well, we tend to draw *moral satisfactions* from it. Moral perspective seems to be a driving force for building narrative identities for oneself or for others.

Further, we may draw a distinction between our *own* sense of selfhood and the narrative identity we construct for *others*. Novitz seems to overlook this distinction. And this is responsible for a certain contradiction in his approach. He does grant that in constructing a narrative self, we have a "moral interest". But a little later, while considering the experience of a lingering feeling of regret about some past failure in life, he remarks that such regret "is not moral, but an aesthetic response to what 'we regard' as a blemished image, a sullied narrative".[1] How are we to reconcile his claim about "moral interest" in narrative self with his later suggestion that to our own "sullied narrative" the response can but only be "aesthetic"? One way to resolve this difficulty would be to recognize the distinction we are drawing attention to.

It is important to keep in mind that the narrative self we construct for conveying it to others is not to be conflated with the sense of selfhood we already have. Selectively taking together certain facts about my life, I may also create my own self-identity. But I may not want to project this sense of selfhood to others and, therefore, construct narrative identities, which could be presented to others. Moreover, repeated attempts to construct my narrative selfhood on different occasions and to present them to different people are carried out with the end in view that my image should favourably fit with the ideals that are held up laudatory by the community or society we live in. This, to my mind, would seem to run counter to the way that a work of art is created. Rather than its conformability to some pre-existent norm or ideal, a work of art is appreciated for its *uniqueness*.[2] A work of art is valued for its "originality" which is to be taken generally to stand for the extent to which it effects a *departure*[3] from the past instances of it. So the parallelism between creating personal narratives and works of art cannot be stretched too far.

Turning to Novitz's argument that the State often develops an interest in what sort of artistic works should be encouraged and patronized, on our view, such an approach could only stifle the creative spirit and may thus be responsible for only mediocrity to thrive. It can hardly be denied that a measure of freedom is the necessary precondition for genuine creativity to manifest itself in terms of *original* works of art. Nor are works of art created primarily for "moral interest" as is the case for constructing narrative identities. On Novitz's own admission, narrative identities "influence" our behaviour and are also linked to the view that we take of the

---

[1] In a different though related context, Anthony O'Hear has the following to say: "Works of art, then, are human creations, made with skill and craft to evoke and express human meanings. They are also and characteristically singular objects, unique in themselves and reflective of one person's intelligence, sensitivity and skill. Even if a work of is reproducible, it cannot be machine-generated, for that will be to undermine the role of the artist and the role of work of are as something intended as such by another human being" (O'Hear 1995, p. 155).

[2] Most of the significant breakthroughs in art may be viewed in perspective as those that are strikingly different from the earlier works.

[3] It is quite another matter that some works of art also convey or transmit a moral message.

behaviour of others. This cannot be said about works of art, for in making them the artist's main concern is not moral but aesthetic (O'Hear 1995, Op Cit. pp. 143–158). While agreeing with Novitz that personal identities are complex structures, which by means of narrative are "constructed" or "invented" rather than discovered, we also contend that these are made primarily for moral, and not aesthetic, purposes. Let me explain the matter clearly. When we create a narrative identity of a character in a literary work of art, we do so keeping in view the other characters and the way they are related to each other. The consideration here is for creating a total structure that would come through as a harmonious whole. There is no such warrant for creating one's own personal identity by means of a narrative about the individual in relation to the others.

6.2   II

And now for a critical understanding of the claim that narrative identities are made quite the way that works of art are created, we would like to draw a distinction between creative structures and mere patterns or designs. This may be elaborated in the following way. Most of the things that are available for use in our consumerist society are marked by their design or pattern, which is primarily linked to the functional efficiency of such object. (Whether it is a toothbrush or an automobile, its design is based on the kind of function it is required to serve.) Design, in this sense, is a rational concept, which is based on the means-end relationship. For example, the best design for a toothbrush would be one that would be most conducive to its smooth and efficient functioning. Even if the appearance or look of a product is taken into consideration while designing it, this must always be subordinated to its functional efficiency. It is important for the production of such objects that their design must be *repeatable*. Thus objects that may look identical can be manufactured in great numbers, but their compact *design* cannot lay claim to their candidature for any serious aesthetic appreciation. All the various machine-made products are only to be treated as so many *instances* of the same design. Repeatability of the same design irrevocably impairs the "singularity" condition, which is a necessary precondition, on Kant's view, for subjecting anything to aesthetic judgement. Pointing to this "tension" between art and technology, Anthony O'Hear convincingly argues that the products of technology, unlike works of art, have no "inner life" (Ayyub 1995, p. 139) of their own, even assuming that technology could perfectly reproduce look-alike art objects. The *inwardness* of work of art invests its structure with a quality that resists any attempt to repeat or reproduce it. On our view, creative *structures* are not repeatable, for they are not made by mere rule following. It is in this respect that we would distinguish creative structures from things that may have been modelled on some *design* based on preconceived plan or set of rules.

This distinction, to our mind, is of crucial importance for our understanding of what narrative identities are like. It must be noted that such identities are constructed on the basis of some *moral ideals* which are either already prevalent in society or are sought to be established for others to follow. The objective here remains that of influencing one's own behaviour or that of others; but in either case the constructed identity implicitly contains a recommendation for future *course of action*. In contrast, the primary objective for which works of art (or creative structures) are created is not to recommend and much less to influence *actions* and *behaviour* in real life. We contend that this vital distinction is overlooked when narrative identities are taken to be similar to creative works of art. This is not to deny that the principles of selectivity and relevancy *are* employed in making narrative identities quite like they are used for the purpose of fashioning out works of art. But for the creative artist, there are no pre-existent norms or models for guiding him to arrive at the end product. Works that are imitative of other artistic creations are not themselves creative. On the other hand, narrative identities even as they are made at the promptings of others *are* identities of sorts all the same. Thus, bringing out the distinction between the moral and the aesthetic, Abu Sayeed Ayyub, in his recently translated book, aptly remarks: "Ethical man, although he is not motivated by self-interest, is nevertheless engaged in action. But the artist is free of the burden of activity and the responsibility of inspiring others to action" (Ayyub 1995). What the artist creates is a world of reality, which is *other than* the reality that surrounds us. But in creating narrative identities, we are not "free of the burden of activity and the responsibility of inspiring others to action" (Ayyub 1995).

Another point that needs some elaboration is with regard to the role of the imagination in creating works of art. We have earlier pointed out that Novitz develops his thesis about narrative identities by arguing that in constructing them we often fall back on the imagination and that this is quite like the way we also create works of art. Now we would not deny that the imagination plays an important role in the construction of narrative selfhoods, for, apart from making certain interpolations, the total configuration of all the details is a product of *imagination*. But, is the use of imagination confined only to making works of art? In our everyday life, we call upon this faculty to come to our help in different situations. For example, a detective who tries to solve a case, a lawyer who builds up defence for his client and a teacher who wants to be effective in the classroom (and so on) all use imagination in their task to achieve the desired end. What then is distinctive about the role of the imagination in the context of art? I think it would be useful to draw here a distinction between, what may be termed, the *substantive* use and the *instrumental* use of the imagination. The latter is instantiated in all the common examples we have cited from everyday life. Imagination, in this sense, has a limited role, which is subordinated to a preset goal. In terms of our examples, the detective wants to prepare a defence for his client which is purported to be based on the *truth* of facts, the teacher wants to find out the *truth* of facts, and the teacher wants to find out the *truth* about how best to get the students in the class interested in his lecture on the chosen topic. Similarly, when we make the narrative identity for presenting it to the others, we also stake our claim (even if implicitly) that it is our *true* identity. (Whether this is really the case is another matter.) The point is that in its limited role (i.e. instrumental use), the imagination is employed to find out what *is* the case or the truth about it. But we would point out that in the context of art, the imagination is used not for finding out what is but rather what *may be possible*. Here, the imagination is used for its own sake and not as an instrument for achieving some other goal. On our view, the imagination finds its *substantive* use only in the context of art. Thus, discussing the role of the imagination in art, Daya Krishna rightly points out:

> In art, the function of the imagination has been primarily conceived as not giving us truth or helping in the exploration of truth, but basically as creating a world which is essentially different from the world as it is actually there. It is, so to say, the creation of a *second order world* which has a reality of its own but which has no relation except that of indirect derivation with the actual world (Krishna 1989, p. 126, emphases added).

This, indeed, is the crux of creative imagination which seeks to transcend the world of facts and delves into the world of emotion and its expressive nature. The imagination holds out the possibility of creating an all together different world which is marked by a degree of transparency as to its internal structure.

The *otherness* of art from life must be deliberately sustained in order that one may respond to art without getting tied down to the parameters within which life must be viewed. Now narrative identities are used for influencing *action* in this world. Far from being removed from life, as is the case with the autonomous status of the work of art, the narrative identity is constructed for the purpose of modifying and transforming *life* by guiding action at different levels, i.e. individual, interpersonal and societal.

Finally, we may turn to the *process* of constructing narrative identities and the *condition* underlying the same. Novitz admits that our freedom in making such narrative is greatly constricted by several factors that among other things include social acceptability, political sanction and inspired perception of the interest of the State. Moreover different interest groups try to impose identities on others who are reduced to being "victims or playthings of the narratives". Narrative identities are used, so it seems, as powerful weapons to control public opinion and perception. In recent times, the role of the media has assumed enormous power for changing and modifying the psyche of the masses for what has been termed as "manufacturing consent".[4] In a social space, which is dotted over with diverse interest groups and power lobbies, it is difficult to imagine there would be enough freedom in the matter of constructing narrative identities without external influences. Such a situation would be quite opposed to the spirit in which any genuine creative activity can take place. Norms and ideals of human behaviour and conduct, if imposed on the individual, will leave him with little choice but to conform his narrative identity to what will be socially acceptable. In contrast, every significant creation must be *unique*, and far from conforming to any pregiven norm or standard, assuming if there be any, it must break with the past instances of art.

This is not to say that the media and other organized channels of public opinion do not try to upheld, transmit and perpetuate certain favoured values and ideals. Hence, Edelman:

---

[4] This has received serious attention from well-known intellectuals of our times, notably Noam Chomsky from whom I have borrowed the term.

In evoking such intellectual and moral outlooks, works of art become far more influential in politics than polemics can be, because they imbue discourse and action with a crucial meaning regardless of what forms these take or how they are rationalized in a particular political arena (Edelman 1995, p. 11)

And:

that art shapes public perception of the legitimacy of the state, public morals, and behaviour: that it is therefore a central influence on support for and opposition to political acts, rulers, and dissidents (Edelman 1995, p. 42)

To be sure, the art scene is bedevilled by attempts to promote the works of certain favoured artists regardless of consideration for the *aesthetic* merit of such works. It is also undeniable that, at least for some people and interest groups, art is a mere commodity that is saleable for securing economic benefits and social influences. Marketability of artworks bring into play political skulduggery that is widely pervasive in all civilized societies. But we need to draw here a distinction between promoting the narrative identity of the artist and evaluating the aesthetic merit of his work of art. When Novitz speaks of the bizarre political machinations in the matter of how works of art come to gain prominence and social respectability, he does not see that often the techniques and strategies for bringing this about fall back on projecting the narrative identity of the *artist* rather than the intrinsic quality of his works. The latter must be able to stand the test of time even if the social acceptability of a work may sometimes be attributable to such aberration in practice.

The process underlying the social acceptability of works of art is one that is often complex with its own vicissitudes as many a time the same work that does not receive much attention during the lifetime of the artist may come into prominence after his death or vice versa. All of this cannot be attributed to the manipulability of critical perception though, as pointed out earlier, the media and other means do sometimes contribute towards this end. What, however, is important is that the creative mind should find it possible to assert over forces from without and create works that are their own justification. The inexorable march of the creative spirit brooks no regimentation in the realm of the imagination that is put to its *substantive* use by the artist. It is true that no work of art is created in a vacuum, as a long tradition must envelop it. But tradition is not to be understood here in the sense of a monotonous continuity of sterile practices and fossilized values. Rather it should be taken in its dynamic conception that will not only assimilate deviations and departures from the past but also spur the creative mind to explore new horizons. Artistic imagination cannot be fettered by the reality of the actual life; it must ever be in search of the *possible* worlds and not be fixed on the truth about the actual.

It is interesting to note here the distinction that Tagore draws between "the world of facts" and "the world of expression". For Tagore, the world of expression—and not the world of facts—demands an emotional empathy with a personal world. The "laws" of the personal world are of the essence of one's creative soul and thus do not appear to be imposed from without. In a sense, even the artist feels overtaken by the tide of the creative process. Tagore, while commenting on the art of painting, says the following:

The art of painting eludes us like a shy mistress and moves along subtle ways — unbe-
known to me. Her ways are such that I am reminded of what the *vedas* say: *kovedah.*
Nobody knows — perhaps not even the creator... It is the tide of creator itself which bears
it along its own current (Neogi n.d., p. 110).

What is true of the pictorial art holds good for other forms of art as well. Tagore's
words bear testimony to the very nature of creative process, which involves a transition from the sense of oppressive facts to the boundless sense of joy by transcending
facts and their laws. To participate in this creative activity is to feel in union with the
principle of rhythmic unity. This process of creative activity is not something cha-
otic, nor is it carried out by adhering to some fixed rules and conventions imposed
from outside. Rather, such process is marked by spontaneity based on a felt unity
with an internal principle of rhythmic harmony.

Now, in constructing narrative identities, we remain far more vulnerable to outside influences to be able to create anything of significance by *free* choice. Contrary
to what obtains in the dynamics of creative activity, making narrative identities in
conformity with the ideals and norms suggested by *others* is the rule rather than the
exception. The reason for this can now be stated clearly enough. For making narrative identities, our interest is *primarily* moral or political and not to seek any aesthetic pleasure from them. In this task, we either imbibe moral ideals and norms
from others to weave them into the narratives we make or want to impose some
ideals on others.

6.3   III

Moral perceptions and concerns that we already share, or want to, with others leave
their imprimatur on the narrative identities we construct for ourselves or for others.
In constructing such identities, we reflect our moral commitment to certain ideals,
though this might involve justifying our own actions on *moral* grounds and even
sometimes denouncing those of others. Novitz, however, likens narrative identities
and the process of their making to that of works of art and the aesthetic process.
This may be true up to a point though not without a significant point of divergence
between the two realms. We cannot ignore the point that the *aesthetic* content of a
work of art is quite independent of any moral message, even if it is argued that such
a work of art may sometimes convey.

Works or art are created primarily for their aesthetic *significance;* judging them
critically is a matter of aesthetic taste and insight. Narrative identities, on the other
hand, are made for the purpose of guiding our *actions* or those of others by focusing
favourably on certain *moral* ideals that underlie such narratives. For this reason, the
parameters for judging narrative identities are moral, *not* aesthetic. The unified
structure of the constructed narratives tends to have stereotypes which draw upon
commonly shared moral perceptions at least within a particular community or society. In the domain of art, stereotypes are always at a discount (even if at all acceptable), for aesthetic creativity must unfold itself into structures that could have no

clones. Now it is quite the case that the characters in a fictional work are defined in terms of narrative identities for which a moral perspective is built into the same. The process is quite like the way we do it in real life by creating narrative identities of people around us or even for one to project one's own identity around others. But this needs to be distinguished from the total narrative structure of the novel or the creative work. Here, the supervening value of the work is to be regarded as aesthetic rather than moral.

However, it must be noted here that the individual narrative structures within a fictional work cannot be divorced from the total narrative structure of the work. The two seem closely related to each other. The question about the relation between morality and aesthetics assumes importance in this context. A fictional work is also necessarily a vehicle of some moral value or perspective though it is not created primarily for this purpose. A literary work is valued mainly for its aesthetic value, but its very narrative structure communicates a distinctive moral message. Interestingly, moral perspective comes into play only in literary works that always have a narrative structure. This is not true of various other forms of art such as abstract painting or tonal music. The point is simple. Where there is no storytelling, there can be no moral message. Literary works of art are predominantly based on storytelling, and so, they carry directly or implicitly a moral message or perspective. For the same reason, great literary works often are those that make us see a moral situation as well as how best to respond ideally to such situations. But these are considered great works not because they contain moral instruction but by virtue of their measure of aesthetic structure and value. We do not read novels or short stories to be instructed in morality or to receive some moral lessons. What is of consequence here is the structure of the literary text and the architecture of emotions that is interwoven into it. The text itself can neither be called moral or immoral. This is so because the content of it is fictional in character and does not lay claim to being part of reality. However, if and when the literary text is published, it may assume a moral dimension in terms of its impact on the reader or the reading public. A parallel case would be with regard to a painting, say that of a nude female figure which may turn into a matter of public controversy as it happened in the case of M.F. Husain's painting of "Bharat Mata". It became a target of public ire as it was taken to represent or depict a real entity. A similar controversy was responsible for banning of *The Satanic Verses* of Salman Rushdie. The point we are making here is that creative literature being in the nature of fiction cannot be characterized as having any moral categories or otherwise. Only when such works are made public or published at a particular point of time or place that moral category may be imputed to it. Another case that comes to mind is that of Taslima Nasreen's novel *Lajja* which was proscribed when it was published some years ago though more recently it has become an occasion for a rethink as is evidenced by the utterances of some prominent political personality. This is not to say that novels, paintings and films are not banned, proscribed or censured. Indeed, they are, and sometimes, with good reasons keeping in considerations their impact on the public or audience.

The foregoing analysis runs counter to the traditionally explicated views of Plato on art and morality in terms of which the immutable moral values epitomize the real world of *Ideas*. Quite understandably, from such a perspective, a creative literary text would divorce the reader from the real world and would have a corrupting influence on the mind of the person. Coming to our own argument, in the first place, a particular character in a novel is not necessarily depiction or representation of a real life character and it is situated in a fictional world. So it makes no sense to impute some moral category to such a character. So the work itself assumes a morally neutral character. Now to extend our point further, when the work is published and put into public domain, we begin to consider the work and the characters in it from our own individual perspective in the light of our moral sensibilities. To put the matter a little differently, when we *read* the literary work, we *find* it and the characters in it as upholding certain moral value or otherwise. The argument predicates itself on the premise that depending on our own moral sensibility and perception, we judge a work or character in it as of certain moral value and, on occasions, worthy of emulation. The crux of the matter is that in an interactive encounter with the narrative text, one brings to bear on it one's own moral understanding and sensibility, thereby refurbishing and sometimes enriching their moral knowledge. But is it necessary for the aesthetic merit of a narrative text to embody or carry forth some moral dimension? This is a pertinent question that has a bearing on the view of the relationship between aesthetics and morality and stands in need of further clarification. Indeed, various positions have been taken on this issue by contemporary thinkers, and some of these may be revisited briefly in order to contextualize our own response to this *matter*.

Towards this end, we may turn to the seminal article "Art, Narrative, and Moral Understanding" by Noel Carroll (2001, pp. 126–160). As rightly pointed out, the oldest and the best known Platonic tradition "situates art in ever-expanding circles of guilt" as "Plato himself chides art for proposing characters who are bad moral role models". He goes on to point out that "It thrives in our humanities departments, where all art works have become the subject of systematic interrogation either for sins of commission – often in terms of their embodiment of bad role models or stereotypes – or for sins of omission – often in terms of people and viewpoints that have been left out" (Carroll 2001, pp. 128) This apart, the basic point of argument against all art (mimetic or nonmimetic) is that it corrupts the mind by inducing emotion and "thereby, undermines the righteous reign of reason in the soul" (Carroll 2001, p. 128). When looked at from this perspective, the world of make-believe emotions is far away from the world of reason which alone can lay claim to the knowledge of immutable moral values. Thus there remains an antagonism between works of art and moral values. Such an approach would seem to give way to critiquing literary works of art for ideally not being a source of moral knowledge.

This position of antagonism between art and morality is contestable from the point of view of Aristotle. For that matter, reason may well be regarded as a constituent of the emotion and not as something that necessarily and always stands in opposition to it. And, as Carroll maintains, so "it is possible to join Aristotle in regarding arts as such and theatre in particular as ways of educating emotions such as pity and fear by means of clarifying them…" (Carroll 2001, p. 131). Since emotions come into play in a literary work of art, they are a means to clarifying, and sometime edifying, our moral perception. Admittedly, such an approach factors in a possible moral dimension while considering literary works of art. Further, the role of literary works of art would seem to be directed to *clarifying* moral sentiments through the narrative. But can that be the basis for the measure of the merit of a literary work of art? Moreover, what parameters would be applicable to judging a text as a literary artwork? These questions do not get resolved on the basis of the view outlined above. True, such an approach admits of literary artworks having a moral content. But this does not take us far in deciding whether they are to be regarded as creative works by virtue of having moral dimension. How are we going to distinguish between imaginative literary works and those that contain moral instruction or propaganda? This problem gets accentuated in yet another kind of approach that has come to be characterized as "utopianism". This is another way of putting forth the thesis that all art must be morally uplifting. However, this is not borne out by our actual encounter with literary artworks. As Noel Carroll says, "Utopianism seems highly improbable. It appears entirely too facile and convenient that the ontology of art should be able to guarantee that all art is morally ennobling" (Carroll 2001, p. 132). Indeed, this is not applicable to all works that are counted as literary artworks. It is not the case that all art is always "morally valuable". So this cannot be turned into the defining criterion of literary arts.

We may now turn to the approach that talks of, as already discussed in an earlier chapter, the autonomy of art. A theory that identifies art with morality would remain a surrogate to its aesthetic merit. While it is true that a literary narrative is likely to have more often than not situations of emotional conflicts as these may be interwoven into its structure, its total form is a closed one marked by a degree of finality that is not given in real life. The finality or closure of the literary form anticipates resolution of emotional conflicts. In this sense, what we experience here is rightly called "virtual life". Moral predicates are inapplicable to this domain of "virtual life" though the reader's response to it could be through the prism of moral perception. However, it is the resolution of the emotional conflict into an attendant "closed" form that is likely to give the reader a sense of satisfaction or delight as of aesthetic nature. So what brings about this sense of satisfaction is the aesthetic form of the narrative structure and not the moral dimension as such. Such an approach does arise from the standpoint of maintaining the "autonomy" of art. An important consideration for holding the autonomy thesis is that there are forms of art in which the form or the formal structure supersedes all other determinants for judging the object of attention as an artwork. For example, an abstract painting or sculpture would demand our attention, or sometime even appreciation, as a work of art. Why we regard such instances as art is only for their formal quality. In such cases, there is no role for a moral dimension to come into play.

The autonomy thesis of art comes for a detailed critical consideration in Noel Carroll's seminal article referred to above. As he puts the position succinctly, for the autonomist "art is essentially independent of morality and politics" and that "aesthetic value is independent of the sort of consequentialist considerations that Plato and his followers raise" (Carroll 2001, p. 120). Further, "Art on the autonomist view is intrinsically valuable, it should not be subservient to ulterior or external or extrinsic purposes, such as producing moral consequences or inducing moral education. For the autonomist, anything devoted to such ulterior purposes could not be art, properly so called" (Carroll 2001, p. 120). However, Noel Carroll comes out with a critique of such an approach. In the first place, he points out that autonomy thesis by its very nature is based on essentialism whereby it precludes the possibility of defining art in terms of anything other than its aesthetic character. In other words, autonomy thesis is an outcome of essentialism which has come under attack by some of the analytic philosophers in the wake of later Wittgenstein such as Morris Weitz, W.B. Gallie, W.E. Kennick and others (as already discussed in Chap. 1). The basic underlying point of anti-essentialism remains that there is no single necessary and sufficient characteristic by which to define art. Instead, what is pressed into service is the Wittgenstein's idea of "family resemblances" among the arts. Quite in line with this idea, Carroll suggests that rather than identifying art with a single determinant, namely, its aesthetic domain, we may look for other necessary characteristics such as moral and political values. In other words, he does not outright reject "autonomism" out of hand but treats it as one of the various determinants of art along with moral and political dimensions. So Carroll declares "I would like to develop a philosophical account – of one of the most important comprehensive relation of art to morality.... But at the same time I will try to develop this account in such a way that it confronts or accommodates the objections of the autonomist" (Carroll 2001, p. 134).

Let us now turn to some of the arguments that Carroll comes up against autonomism. He looks to the past and argues that historically speaking art was not completely divorced from religion, social activities and political goals. Consequently, most of these works of art have a strong moral dimension. More importantly, he argues that these works can be interpreted, understood and appreciated only in terms of their moral dimensions. So:

> To understand a literary work, for instance, generally requires not only that one use one's knowledge of ordinary language and verbal associations, drawn from every realm of social activity and valuation, but also, most frequently, that *audiences deploy many kinds of everyday reasoning, including moral reasoning, simply to understand the tex*t. How can the negative claims of autonomism – that art is divorced from every other realm of social praxis – be sustained in such a way as to render literary communication intelligible? (Carroll 2001, 135, our italics)

Here, Carroll perhaps is making an important point in as much as he is underlining the process of *interpreting* and *understanding* the literary text with the *help* of moral reasoning. But this argument does not go very far in demolishing the claims of autonomism. True, we often are able to understand and make sense of the novel by attending to its moral dimension. True, without understanding a narrative artwork, we would not be in a position to appreciate the work. But this is not to say that the primary purpose and function of the artwork is to impart moral knowledge. Notwithstanding the moral dimension, we would appreciate and evaluate the work on the basis of its aesthetic merit. A novel, for example, may not be regarded as a good narrative artwork even if it contains valuable moral message. On the other hand, a literary artwork may be upheld as a specimen of good work even though it may have no significant moral reasoning or message. Samuel Beckett's *Waiting for the Godot* could be considered as a case in point. Surely, we *understand* a literary artwork better by understanding its moral reasoning just as we would contend that we understand a text only by understanding the word meanings in it. But from this it does not follow that understanding the moral message in a text determines our judgment as to whether or not it may claim to be a literary artwork.

Further, historically it may be unexceptionably true to claim that so much narrative art was created under the influence of religious, social, political and moral ideas. But how does it follow from this that the aesthetic merit of the work would depend on these considerations? Understanding a piece of moral reasoning is not the same as experiencing aesthetic satisfaction. It is one thing to say that a good novel may make us also understand some moral contention but quite another to say that it is a good narrative artwork *by virtue of* the same. Noel Carroll's argument falls short of such a conclusion. It is a kind of reductionism to hold that whatever is interesting or even satisfying in terms of a moral message or dimension would also *necessarily* be aesthetically satisfying. Conversely, some artworks that are aesthetically satisfying may also contain moral dimension. Literary artworks usually deal with human situations, actions, responses and emotions that relate to a make-believe created world. By virtue of its "virtual" nature the "closed" form of the literary work, it has a kind and degree of transparency that is not to be found in our real life and world. The complex web of human actions and emotions seem closely interrelated to one another. The reader while going through the literary work seeks to interpret and understand the actions and emotions in a contrived moral domain. This perhaps is what is suggested by Noel Carroll when we argue that the literary work becomes intelligible through the intervention of moral categories. For Carroll, "When reading a novel or viewing a drama, our moral understanding is engaged already. Reading a novel, for example, is itself generally a moral activity insofar as reading narrative literature typically involves us in a continuous process of moral judgment, which continuous exercise of moral judgment itself can contribute to the expansion of our moral judgment" (Carroll 2001, p. 145). But we would argue that to construe it as an evaluative category, to our mind, cannot claim to be its logical corollary even if we admit that in some recognized cases of literary art, we may *also* appreciate the moral dimension.

Carroll's critiquing of autonomism is premised on his view of anti-essentialism that brooks no common denominator theory. Yet he seems to contradict his position when he advocates, as he seems to do for the most part, moral dimension in all narrative works to be a *necessary* component for their excellence. One can raise here the legitimate question, is morality the defining characteristic of all narrative artworks? An affirmative answer to this question would imply an essentialist position—one that comes under attack by Noel Carroll in his attempt to destabilize the autonomist's thesis.

However, it would be well to remind ourselves that Carroll does not altogether reject the basic tenet of autonomism as he clearly admits that it "rides on the unexceptionable observation that art appears to aim, first and foremost, at being absorbing. The so-called aesthetic experience is centripetal. Thus, if the artwork essentially aims at our absorption in it, then it is valuable for its own sake" (Carroll 2001, p. 136). Please note the sceptical manner in which he speaks of the "so-called aesthetic experience" as for a philosopher of analytic persuasion, the talk about aesthetic experience is perhaps nothing but a red herring. As brought out earlier, the analytic philosopher who is averse to making a reference to aesthetic experience would be open to the charge of "psychologism". Autonomism, for sure, invokes the essential association of artworks with aesthetic experience which the analytic philosopher finds it difficult to characterize in *objective* terms, and so, it remains a bone of contention. Carroll's position, to our mind, remains ambivalent on the claims of autonomism while not rejecting outright at the same time substituting it for the appreciation of moral dimension in respect of *some* cases of narrative artworks.

Now it is nobody's case that at least in the case of some well-acknowledged literary works, we do *also* appreciate the moral dimension that is at play. But this is not to detract us from appreciating the work on its aesthetic ground. Once the aesthetic nature of the artwork is established, the other domains such as moral, social or political get subsumed under the same. The point is that the primary purpose of creating artworks is its aesthetic appreciation though while acknowledging this, one may also read into them moral or political ideas and reasoning. The basic quarrel of analytic philosophers like Carroll and others is with the kind of essentialism that is entailed by autonomism. While they might grant that some artworks may be upheld on purely aesthetic grounds, they want to hold that some other works are to be upheld purely on moral grounds. They seem to miss or overlook the point that autonomism stands for an inclusive approach and is bedrock for subsuming under it various other values and categories. An aesthetically satisfying work may also open out moral dimensions such as to contribute to a greater sense of enhancement and enrichment for the reader. In what way does such a position seek to demolish autonomism? By trying to do so in the article under reference, Noel Carroll binds himself in knots of ambiguity and contradiction. This is borne out by what he says towards the end of his article. In his own words:

> It is *not the function* of a narrative artwork to provide moral education. Typically, the purpose of a narrative artwork is to absorb the reader, viewer, or listener.... *The autonomist is correct in denying that narrative art necessarily serves such ulterior purposes as moral education.* Nevertheless, that does not preclude their being moral reasoning with respect to narrative artworks. (Carroll 2001, p. 154 our italics)

And, a little later, he concludes the article as follows:

> Moreover, contra autonomism, since narrative artworks are *designed to enlist moral judgment and understanding,* morally assessing such works in light of the quality of the moral experience they afford is appropriate. (Carroll 2001, p. 155 our italics)

It is quite evident here that what he says in conclusion does not follow from what he says a little earlier. He seems to be caught in a warp of ambiguity and contradiction. Indeed, we are quite in agreement with his statement that "it is not the function of a narrative artwork to provide moral education" (p 155). But how does it follow from this to claim that "narrative artworks are designed to enlist moral judgment and understanding" (p. 155). In our view, the argument does not hold good. We certainly quite agree with his statement that the function of a narrative artwork is to provide moral education, but not with his later statement that these are designed to enlist moral judgment and understanding. A literary artwork stands or falls on the basis of the aesthetic ground alone. It is another thing that while we appreciate its aesthetic quality, we also discern some moral concern or reasoning in some of the works. It is important to understand that a narrative literary artwork involves storytelling by selectively putting together characters, situations, emotions and responses all of which are integral to the work. The narrative structure is also an organic whole in which all these elements are transparently related to one another. So there would always be an occasion for considering some moral concern as one makes sense of the story or the plot. But this would at best be in the nature of an epiphenomenon rather than being the heart of its aesthetic structure. So the talk about moral concern in the context of a literary work would be quite natural but would not detract one from appreciating the aesthetic merit of the artwork. Quite justifiably, we would hold on to the distinction between the aesthetic domain and the moral concern, and the two should not be conflated. Works of art are upheld as good or bad on the basis of their aesthetic quality and not for their moral content or reasoning. It is another matter that alongside appreciating the aesthetic merit of a literary artwork, one may also refer to the moral concern and reasoning and their effective use in the work, thereby giving the reader an occasion to appreciate the same in a given situation.

Indeed, aesthetic view of a work does not preclude the possibility of appreciation of the attendant moral dimension which may be present in many literary works. It does not follow from this that we could abandon autonomism in favour of holding moral concern as determinant of art. Carroll's point about the moral basis of making artworks goes against the very grain of creativity. Nor does his anti-essentialist stance in critiquing autonomism hold much water since it is premised on the belief that it is just *one of the ways of* looking at art alongside several *other ways* of looking at art. Autonomism, by definition, excludes all other ways of characterizing art. So autonomism that stands for the view of "Art for Art's sake" does not brook any other competing theory of art. How can Carroll hybridize autonomism with his view of "Art for the sake of moral knowledge"? The two standpoints apparently are mutually exclusive of each other. This is not to say that works of art do not admit of a moral dimension. Indeed, often moral concern may play itself out as integral to its aesthetic denouement. But this cannot claim to be its basic point of attention. Determining the claim of a narrative text as a literary artwork on the consideration of its underlying moral concern would be to subscribe to a surrogate theory of art. This is comparable to the case of a piece of music that is set to some lyrics, but the musical merit owes itself only to the tonal structure and not its lyrics or theme though the latter may come for appreciation as an integral part of it.

Our main concern in this chapter has been to refute the analytic philosopher's standpoint with regard to the claim that narrative works are vehicles of moral concern and knowledge by virtue of which they could claim to be literary artworks. We have argued that in terms of autonomism, the literary artwork is primarily appreciated on aesthetic ground to the extent that it absorbs our attention and thereby gives us a special kind of satisfaction. The view that it may also be a source of moral or political ideas cannot be regarded as a determining characteristic of its aesthetic merit. Those who advance such a view fail to account for the primary purpose for which literary artworks are created. No doubt every narrative artwork has a story to tell in which actions, responses, emotions and situations come into play. Quite obviously, there would also be a certain perspective that would be required to weave together all the details into a well-structured story. A literary work written, for example, from a feminist viewpoint would bring forth the plight of the woman protagonist in a misogynistic society. So the reader is quite likely to read into the text the feminist ethics. A critical appreciation of such a work would not allow the reader to remain untouched by the moral and ethical dimensions of the situation. Similarly, a lot of *Dalit* or subaltern literary works stand for social reformative practices. Thus it is quite fashionable to classify literature into Black literature, subaltern literature, feminist literature, postcolonial literature and so on. True, the importance of many of these works is to impart sensitivity for the reader to view and understand the contemporary social matrix in life. It gives us a deeper understanding of the trials and tribulations of human life and existence. Yet, this is not the primary function of creating narrative works of art since the basic impulse for creativity is to present a narrative structure that would be interesting, absorbing and satisfying as an experience. Defining the literary work in terms of how it influences an individual reader or a community of readers in various different ways is to commit what has come to be known as "affective fallacy". The determining condition for regarding some narrative structure as an artwork is the degree to which it is capable of giving us such satisfaction. How else does the work affect the reader is incidental to such aesthetic satisfaction. And what accrues as an incidental cannot be construed into a defining characteristic of a narrative artwork.

Integral to this is the issue of State or government censorship of literary works which sometimes goes to the extent of banning a work. Salman Rushdie's *Satanic Verses* and Taslima Nasreen's *Lajja* exemplify such approach. Obviously, the underlying rationale for such censorship relates to moral reasoning and concern. The assumption is that such works may have an insalubrious effect on the reader or hurt the sensibilities of a particular class of readers. It is often overlooked that literary artworks are fictional in nature and not mere record of facts or factual situations. Also, one must draw a distinction between good and bad literary works such that good ones appeal only to one's aesthetic sensibility. Only when a work lacks aesthetic sensibility it may draw attention to other extra-aesthetic concerns. A work may act as a surrogate for being a source of historical information or moral knowledge which in turn may be regarded as incorrect or pernicious. In a good or successful work of literary art, its aesthetic sensibility to absorb the reader's attention supervenes over other considerations that may accrue from it. This also lends credence to our standpoint that a literary artwork primarily appeals to our aesthetic sensibility notwithstanding other considerations such as social, moral, historical inputs. It is important to remember that storytelling is involved in all narrative artworks which is essentially fictional in character and no truth value can be applied to the same. What is thus created is an ideal world or a mental construct of the storyteller. It presents a closed form in which all the different elements such as characters, situations, events, responses and emotions are all related in a way such that every element is relevant to the total construal. To the reader it is the form or the way the story develops or is told that is absorbing and appeals to their aesthetic sensibility. In the process one may also respond to the moral concern or dimension that holds the story together. So the moral knowledge that one gleans out from the story is only by way of a by-product and not something for which we respond to the work primarily. The domain of the aesthetic must not be conflated with that of the moral though the latter is not antithetical to the aesthetic value.

References

Ayyub, Abu Sayeed. (Tr.). (1995). Amitava Ray, *Modernization and Tagore*, Sahitya Akademi, New Delhi.

Carroll, N. (2001). Art, narrative, and moral understanding. In J. Levinson (Ed.), *Aesthetics and ethics: Essays at the intersection*. Cambridge: Cambridge University Press.

Edelman, M. (1995). *From art to politics: How artistic creation shape political conceptions*. Chicago: University of Chicago Press.

Krishna, D. (1989). Arts and the cognitive enterprise of man. In *The art of the conceptual: Explorations in a conceptual maze over three decades*. Delhi: ICPR.

Neogi, P. (ed) *Rabindranath Tagore on art and aesthetics: A selection of lectures, essays, and letters,*

Novitz, D. (April 1989). Art, narrative and human nature. *Philosophy and Literature, 13*.

O'Hear, A. (1995). Art and technology: An old tension. In R. Fellows (Ed.), *Philosophy and technology*. Cambridge, MA: Cambridge University Press.

Printed in Great Britain
by Amazon

36461468R00057